GRACE FOR GRACE.

LETTERS

OF

REV. WILLIAM JAMES.

"And of His fulness have all we received, and grace for grace."—JOHN i: xvi.

NEW YORK:

DODD & MEAD, PUBLISHERS,

762 BROADWAY.

"Lovest thou me!" I hear my Saviour say.
Would that my heart had power to answer, "Yea,
Thou knowest all things Lord, in heaven above
And earth beneath, Thou knowest that I love."
But 'tis not so, in word, in deed, in thought;
I do not, cannot love Thee as I ought.
Thy love must give the power, Thy love alone,
There's nothing worthy of Thee but Thine own.
Lord, with the love wherewith Thou lovest me,
Reflected on Thyself, I would love Thee.

MONTGOMERY.

PREFACE.

THE theme of these letters is the life of God in the soul, as it is imparted, nourished, strengthened, and perfected, by His abounding grace. They treat of the most intimate and vital relations of the believer with Christ; of the reception of the Redeemer into the heart by a simple and appropriating faith; of His sufficiency and power, when thus received, to free the soul from the sense of condemnation, and from the intolerable and hopeless struggle for self-deliverance, and to establish it in the peace, joy, and victory of an assured and realized salvation. The mission of sorrow, especially of spiritual trial, in the accomplishment of this Divine purpose, is most clearly illustrated and unfolded, as are also those profound views of the nature of sin, and of holiness, which the depth and intensity of Mr. James's convictions rendered peculiarly vivid.

The letters have been selected from the private correspondence which Mr. James held with many friends, and which he often continued through a long series of years, with wonderful persistency of sympathy and fullness of blessing. As it is supposed that the reader will be more interested in the thoughts communicated than in the extreme personality often associated with their expression, passages harmonious in substance and aim have sometimes been combined, and thus are not always given in the exact connection in which they were written.

Yet as very much of Mr. James's personal experience is interwoven with all of his free and informal correspondence, it should be remembered that his deeper inward and individual life was always thus revealed, not in egotism, but in generous response to the solicitations of those to whom he wrote. Animated by the desire, which with him was so absorbing, to do his utmost for the encouragement and welfare of others, he hesitated not to record, not only his victories, but his errors and defeats, if he might hope, by pointing out their causes and their meaning, to sustain or rescue some struggling soul passing through similar dangers and trials.

If any desire to know more of his rare characteristics and varied gifts, they will find, in an appendix, extracts from a brief but most appreciative memorial prepared by Rev. Henry Neill, soon after Mr. James's death in 1868, which was published more especially for circulation among his personal friends, in connection with two sermons written by him, one of which gave the title to the book, "The Marriage of the King's Son." It contained also two of his letters, and quotations from others, which, together with the selections from the memorial, are included (with the kind consent of the biographer, and of the publisher, A. D. F Randolph) in this volume.

The present collection of letters is mainly due to the numerous and earnest requests which those holding them in their possession have received, that they would give them a fuller and more extended publication. Another strong incentive has arisen from the fact that Mr. James was engaged with intense enthusiasm, during his later years, upon a work to which he brought all the treasures gathered in a lifetime from devout study, from rare spiritual discovery, and from the practical experience of a nature rich in feeling and profoundly receptive of Divine communications. The subject of this work was that which also runs through nearly all of his personal correspondence, viz.: What Christ does for the fallen soul in the way of redemption and conquest, and how the soul can obtain the sanctifying effects that flow from His salvation.

Mr. James often alludes to this as the crowning interest of his life, in writing to his friends, and in connection with it says: "Certainly no sojourner in the desert of Sinai was ever more exercised about setting his foot upon the land of promise than I have been, I might almost say for forty years, about leading a chosen band out of the wilderness of legal and worldly temptation to that glorious inheritance which is described by the term Sanctification."

But the Master's call summoned him, as it did the noble leader of the Israelites, to the glories and rewards of the Heavenly Canaan before he saw the accomplishment of his cherished hope in the way he had looked for. Yet may we not believe that the same blessed truths to which he so ardently desired to give abundant utterance, will, through these letters, reach and deliver many a wanderer in the desert and in the wilderness, the more effectually, it may be, because they were written, not so much to establish a doctrine as to meet the wants of individual souls, with the advantage, also, of being warmed and lighted by personal experience.

The letters have been classified as definitely as the nature of their contents would allow. The brief quotations from Mr. James's own words, together with a few confirming texts of Scripture, which precede the different sections, will give an idea of their subjects, though they are all attuned to the same inspiring strain which underlies and unites them all in its Divine harmony—the free, unbounded, changeless love of God, which saves, purifies, sanctifies, and glorifies the soul. Indeed, the key-note of Mr. James's instruction, and hope, and holiest living, may be expressed in one of his own comprehensive sentences: "I am a firm believer in the Omnipotence of Love."

May many who are thirsting for the living waters drawn from "the wells of salvation," find these letters very rich and deep channels of blessing.

S. W. H.

SECTION I.

THE GIFT OF GRACE.

FREE JUSTIFICATION AND FULL SALVATION THROUGH CHRIST THE REDEEMER.

"FOR by grace are ye saved through faith; and that not of yourselves: it is the gift of God."—Ephesians ii. 8.

* * * * * The first real conception of grace is the germ of your deliverance. "The gift of God is eternal life through Jesus Christ our Lord." The first practical apprehension of this truth is the believer's starting point, its growth and confirmation is the main end of the Divine discipline, and our progress, perseverance, and final victory depend simply on keeping hold of it.

"Therefore being justified by faith we have peace with God through our Lord Jesus Christ: by whom also we have access by faith into this grace wherein we stand."—Romans v. 1, 2

* * * * * Justification is absolute and free. It is simply an act of grace which rescues us at once and forever from all the penalties of law, and insures the Divine mercy through all the changes of our everlasting being. Less than this would not be an adequate expression of Infinite love, nor an adequate exponent of the value of Christ's sacrifice.

"Where sin abounded grace did much more abound: that as sin reigned unto death, even so might grace reign through righteousness unto eternal life, by Jesus Christ our Lord."—Romans v. 21, 22.

GRACE FOR GRACE.

SECTION I.

THE GIFT OF GRACE.

FREE JUSTIFICATION AND FULL SALVATION FOR THE SOUL THROUGH CHRIST THE REDEEMER

I.

YOUR last call pierces even to the seat of tears. That ceaseless plaint " How long, how long," is always in my ears, and compels me to write, hoping that I may give you some new strength. My Saviour will not suffer me to be deceived, nor to deceive you in this matter. All you want is strength, and that is coming—only in a way quite contrary to that in which you are probably looking for it. I had better have said, perhaps, that what you radically need is a stronger evangelical illumination. It seems too simple to say and yet there cannot be a doubt that what you want above everything, and as inclusive of everything, is more faith in Christ.

I feel certain that you have a very true and living conviction of the spirituality of the law of God, and consequently of the strength of indwelling sin. I wish I could say that you are as sound and thorough in your evangelical experience as you are in your legal. But here lies your great difficulty,—the source, in my apprehension, of all your spiritual weakness. While you can say with as much moral earnestness as any one, "wretched man that I am, who shall deliver me,—" you cannot say with any perfect assurance, "I thank God through Jesus Christ."

You tell me, "I want to believe in Jesus Christ just as the Holy Spirit who dictated the command would have me." I cannot but think from this expression, connected with my general knowledge of our nature (not of yours in particular), that it is one of your great faults, as it is one of mine, to look more at yourself than at Christ,—to rely more on some quality in your own faith than on His love and faithfulness and power. To believe in Christ just as the Holy Spirit would have you, is to trust in Him absolutely, and without reference to anything in yourself but your wants, weaknesses, sins, and miseries. If you do not find that answer to your faith which you were looking for, this should only determine you to trust more simply, and to trust forever, leaving it to God to give you at present just what He pleases, but never doubting that He will give you at last all that He has promised. I have lived in this way now for a good while, and I can testify that it makes a difference. I find that what hurts me in any state is an expectation of something in *it* or from it which I should expect only in and from God. I have no more expectation of being better from anything I find in myself, but my expectations enlarge and become firmer constantly as the result of trusting only and wholly in Him. No language can tell the depth of my misery and helplessness on any other principle. I am entirely bankrupt, but I have a Surety. There is no reason why we should not be just as certain of our salvation as we are of our ruin. Christ is a *perfect* Redeemer. His work is a unit. The love which carried Him to the cross, where He stood between us and eternal condemnation, secures every spiritual influence which is needful to complete our deliverance.

The only condition of justification is faith; and this is a condition only in the sense that *trusting*, in all our lower relations, is the condition of harmony in those relations. There is no merit in it. In the nature of things the love of God can be of no benefit to us unless we believe it,—the great sacrifice of no advantage unless we rely upon it.

Faith is the necessary action of the soul that wants life, and that believes, though conscious of utter demerit, on God's testimony in the Scriptures alone, that He for Christ's sake can and will give it. I am very anxious to guard your mind against those loose ideas of the nature of faith which represent it as something which gives as well as takes. There is much confounding of what the old divines call Legal Repentance—an exercise which, from the nature of things, precedes faith and prepares for it, with that consecration of the soul to God which follows faith. The former is simply the product of self-love—an earnest desire of deliverance from an evil which threatens our destruction—an act to which we are constrained not by love but by law; a very different act in its nature from that which follows a true faith, wherein by the power received from Him we yield ourselves wholly and joyfully to God. Though these two acts are indeed as inseparable as the two operations by which we exhale the fetid breath of our own system, and inhale the pure air of God's atmosphere, yet it is a legal gospel which tells you that you can give anything acceptable to God until you have first received from Him. The disposition to give, or to consecrate one's self to God is no part of the essence of faith. It is the effect of faith.

The very thing you are seeking—the whole thing you are seeking, is the *power* of yielding yourself wholly to God. There never was an expression which more perfectly contains the pith and substance of the Gospel, than the famous one of St. Augustine, " Give what Thou commandest, and then command what Thou wilt." Under the law, we are forever trying to give something to God as a condition of receiving something from Him. Very certainly where faith is strong, that is where there is a very clear perception of Christ's love and work, there cannot but be a consciously responsive action of the soul in giving all to Him ;

but to talk of this last as being an exercise of faith, and thus a condition of life, when it is so evidently the love which is the fruit of faith—the love which faith works, shows a zeal for the law which is not according to knowledge. Depend upon it, the fullness and entireness of your consecration to God, will always be in proportion to the freeness and fullness with which you first receive from Him.

I am very earnest on this subject, because that the mixing of giving and receiving in the act of faith was my great error for a long period, and the very error from the influence of which I am extremely anxious to deliver you. Nothing is more obstructive to the life of the soul, and nothing that I have ever learned so greatly helps its progress as to be in this matter so clearly delivered. Salvation in all its parts has already been purchased for you—made legally yours—willed to you by the testament of your dying Lord—and you have nothing to do but to appropriate it. This and this only is faith.

"As many as *received* Him to them gave He power to become the sons of God, even to them that believe on His name." We may say that as far as spiritual strength or freedom is concerned, that is the cardinal doctrine of Christianity.

My dear friend, all that you need is simply an inward light which shall reveal to you the fullness of Christ, and the relations of perfect freedom in which you stand to it—a taking the veil from your mind which prevents your clearly understanding, or strongly grasping the meaning of the Scriptures, by which you will see in a moment, that you have been like Hagar in the wilderness, perishing with thirst, while by a single touch of the angel an exhaustless fountain was within reach of her eye.

II.

YOUR letter has reached me safely—a precious letter to me, making me much better acquainted with your religious feelings, and both by the natural and the Christian traits which it displays greatly increasing the interest you had before awakened. I loved you from the first as Christ loved the young man, before the test had been applied by which they were separated. I love you now as He loved the Mary who had "chosen the good part which could not be taken from her." How many spiritually disposed young persons there are on the outer circle of the great worldly vortex, who might be saved the saddest experiences of life, if one strong friend, fully understanding their situation, would devote himself to their rescue.

You want to be saved from a vain and worldly life, of which all persons at your age and with your ardent temperament are in great danger. You feel that you will find a help in my friendship in proportion as it serves to defend you against those tides of secularizing care and excitement which were drifting you away from the end of your highest aspirations. You are sick of the hollowness of a worldly or a merely natural life, and you are charmed with the idea of a state of purity in which your affections will find just what they were made for. This is the idea of the salvation which through Christ is attainable by all who desire it, however conscious at present of their destitution of every other qualification. The greatest obstruction to your progress (supposing real earnestness), will arise from the tendency of your mind—not peculiar to you—to be forever looking within to see what has been gained. I wish you could see that this in Christians can proceed from nothing but distrust of the Saviour. This is *unbelief*, and will prove the source of all your discouragement and perplexity. On the contrary, if you can only get the habit of constantly meditating on, or referring to the perfection of Christ as a Saviour, thinking of those Scriptures which relate to this point, and using them in prayer with application to yourself; if you can get the habit of making all your barrenness and backwardness but a stronger reason for trusting Him (for which the Scriptures give you the most abundant warrant), you will find the greatest advantage in it. Learn to feel that your salvation in all its parts is already *secured* by His love, and you have nothing to do but always simply and entirely to trust Him, no matter what objections an evil conscience may raise. You have heard much of union with Christ, from which everything good flows. It is by the exercise of this habit of trusting alone that this union becomes after a while a matter of consciousness,—and then, when we have been so thoroughly tried that no danger can result from the discovery of good in ourselves, such good begins to appear without our looking for it. You never will find it in any other way.

The want of faith or confidence in Christ is the root of all our difficulties. In every genuine work of grace this confidence is a principle of slow growth, and its increase can come only from God. The basis of such a work is a thorough knowledge of ourselves, and in this there is everything to weaken and perplex us. Health, (where there is latent disease), can only come through feeling our sickness; knowledge, through a consciousness of ignorance; holiness, through a sense of sinfulness. As the invalid, greatly diseased, is often distressed by the fear that he can never recover, at least to perfect soundness, and the mind toiling with its rudeness that it can never reach a high degree of culture—so it is, and much more so, with the soul that seeks after a perfect union with God. I would not think much of a Christian life of which a consciousness of great difficulty was not a principal element: and yet, I confess, there is another view of the matter which makes it wonderful that there should ever be any difficulty at all. When we consider the freeness and abundance of the Divine promises, their source in the unchanging goodness of the Divine nature, and the additional security for their fulfillment which we have in the work which Christ has done for us, and in the love, the special love which He has for the weak and ruined and miserable, it is amazing that we should have any doubt at all.

I have got upon a theme which I might pursue without end. But God only by His Spirit can make you apprehend it,—and therefore I shall only commend you to Him, and advise you to pray and wait, and wait and pray, till He shall show this glorious mystery. If I can only be the means of leading you to Christ, or of putting you in the way of finding Him, the end of all my desires and all my efforts for you will be fully answered. The ideas which I present may not be new to you, but the Spirit of God may bring them home to your heart, and will, whenever your necessities demand it, with such an increase of life and power as may make you think you never knew before what it was to believe in Christ. A single passage of Scripture may be blessed to make you learn more in an hour than you have learned in all your life before. While you are engaged in prayer, or engaged in any way (only inwardly waiting on God), a thought may occur to you which will give you the power at once and forever to overcome all difficulties. You may be sure you will not have to wait too long. Your Saviour is infinitely more interested in your success than you are yourself. He will not fail to make that manifest to you at the proper time. You have nothing to do but to cling to Him. Your whole success in the Christian life depends on the clearness and strength with which you are enabled to apprehend that Christ loved you, and having given *Himself* for you, will give you everything else which you need for complete deliverance. Suffer nothing then to diminish your desire, or to embarrass your expectation. "Hope unto the end for the grace that is to be brought unto you at the revelation of Jesus Christ," and stake all on His promises.

Above all, seek constantly those secret communications of light and strength which are given in answer to humble persevering prayer. There is nothing that I ask for in your behalf with so much earnestness, as that you may be enabled to continue in prayer. I know it to be the sole condition of your spiritual growth and fruitfulness. Two things are alternately working to make us negligent here,—despondency, and presumption. "What is the *use* of such prayers as mine," is the suggestion of despondency,—"where is the *need*," is the suggestion of presumption. Be influenced by neither. No matter how low your state,—how overwhelming your consciousness of unfitness for communion with the Holy One, let the thought of His mercy so infinite, as much above our conceptions of it as the heavens are above the earth, sweetly constrain you to cast all your cares upon Him. You will often find—you will generally find Him most near to you when you think Him most distant. On the other hand, be not deceived by any appearances of security. You may fall as suddenly and strangely as you may rise. Trust in the Lord alone—trust Him alike in all circumstances. Let prayer become the one only indispensable habit of your life. Before it gets to be so, you will probably have to overcome a number of delusory ideas, more than I have time now even to enumerate. But be sure there is no delusion, nor uncertainty, in the idea that "prayer is the Christian's vital breath." Thus continue in prayer, and I have no more faith in the Gospel than I have that in a little while you will be going forward, your path all sunshine, and your soul all joy with its bright manifestation.

III.

YOU doubtless remember how strongly you affirmed in a late conversation which we had together, that there was a real difference between us in respect to soul matters. Though I felt myself the difference at the time, I was not prepared then to go fully into its nature; but in reflecting since upon many things which I have heard you say, I am strongly impressed with the belief that I may do you some service by defining the difference as it strikes my own mind.

I trust you will pardon the boldness of my speech if I say that I have no doubt our whole real difference arises from the fact that your natural stock of self-confidence is not quite so nearly exhausted as mine is, and the consequence is, that you are yet *working* for your life—I am more simply *believing* for mine.

Of course, I mean comparatively. My faith is far enough from being as simple as it may be, nor do I mean to say that your working is simply legal

But, do you depend entirely on the sufficiency of Christ? Do you not still feel that you can do something, and that you have something yet *to do*, before you can be assured of your final and everlasting salvation,—and hence are you not constantly looking for evidence in your Christian character to sustain your hope of that glorious consummation?

Without saying at present to what extent I have such assurance, I can say with certainty that what I have rests upon quite another foundation. Our young friend is quite wrong, whom you represent as saying, that I depend on *evidences* for the support of my hope as much as he and you do,—the only difference between us being that while he regards the whole sphere of duty as furnishing the evidence of Christian character, I depend entirely on the evidence which arises out of my secret transactions with Christ. If he had said, that in virtue of my secret transactions with Christ, I had discovered another and more certain way of obtaining assurance, it would have been nearer the truth.

And now let me explain to you what doubtless you are most interested to know, viz., what this better method is, and how I came to it. For a great part of my religious life I have walked, if not in darkness, in a most uncomfortable twilight. I am not sure whether at any particular time the love of Christ or the fear of personal loss was the principal element of the burden; for deficient as I have always felt myself to be, I have seldom been without certain emotions which have appeared like love to Christ and desire for holiness. Still however the hope of doing something which would clear away this disastrous twilight and establish my title to the full enjoyment of Christian privileges, was for a long time the animating principle of my religious life; and all its troubles on the other hand have arisen from my failures to do that thing, or to acquire that character, upon which as I supposed my title, or the assurance of it rather, depended. After trying this way for a much longer time than I hope you will have to do, I was compelled at last to the conclusion that neither assurance nor any other kind of spiritual growth was in that way attainable. My conscience acquitted me on one point. It told me distinctly enough that I had done everything which mortal strength could do, and yet it told me just as clearly that I was not one whit a better man than I was when the struggle began. My intellect had been expanded, and my emotions perhaps had become deeper, but the spirit of self-denying obedience was not more steady, and my temptations were as invincible as ever. At any time I would have been most willing to terminate the conflict by giving up the world if I knew how to do it,—how to get it out of my heart. The things which I would, I did not, and the things which I hated, those I did. I felt myself a miserable captive sold under sin. I saw no way of deliverance but by some Divine manifestation which would completely win my affections. But I had the idea also that this manifestation was in some way conditional upon some act of my own will,—upon an entire self-surrender. How often and long have I labored to do that thing—hoping that the happy hour was not distant when I should do it so thoroughly that God would withhold Himself no longer, and then I should be free! But that hour never came. I never became conscious of surrendering all to God until some time after I had become perfectly assured that God had freely given Himself to me. But understand what I mean by this. I do not mean until God had revealed Himself to me in a personal manner, but I had become practically convinced and settled in the doctrine that the love of God was a fountain for humanity; free in all its fullness, to every one who desired it; that nothing at all was required to make it mine; that it was mine now in virtue of what Christ had done for me, to which nothing could be added by any act of mine whatever. It was simply the principle of *justification by faith alone*, which means, when fully understood, that God's love is always wholly irrespective of our character or of our love to Him.

But what is the effect of this view of the freeness of salvation? It compels me to do as a matter of delight, what I never could do as a matter of duty. I surrender all to God as naturally as I breathe, not as condition of receiving something from Him, for in Christ, and with Christ, I am now persuaded, He has given me everything. This is the doctrine which brought me out of my first bondage; and every step which I have taken since towards a higher freedom, has been impelled by a fresh sense of it, coming to me, for the most part, not when conscious of fidelity to Him, but when most conscious of incurable faithlessness—incurable by any efforts of mine. The utter failure of all my own efforts to do anything for my own cure, and the repeated experience of God's forgiving mercy and tender interest in me notwithstanding, have, at length, broken the power of legality entirely. I see plainly that I shall be saved in spite of myself. The love of God in freely justifying me through the merits of Christ, the love of Christ in dying for me, awakens the strongest desires for holiness, leads to the most earnest, importunate prayers for a better life, works in me resolutions and endeavors which the law-mixture never has done, nor could do. * * * * In view of the Scripture testimonies concerning the way of salvation by Christ, "In whom we have redemption through His blood, the forgiveness of sins according to the riches of His grace," it seems as hard to believe that God will condemn a soul that trusts in Him, as it is under the power of a raging conscience to believe that He will not do it.

My dear brother, let us appropriate Christ's redemption with simplicity. Let every fear lead us to more earnest prayer; that will certainly lead to more illumination, and that to a clearer faith, and a higher consciousness of love, and to a purer life. * * * * * I have much to say to you intensively. You are my brother in a deep sense. Our time relations are dear, but our spiritual relations are much more so. You are one of those of whom I think as eternal companions. In the sense of the ideas of Paul, you are indeed "my beloved and longed for."

IV.

WITH what delight and joy I read your last letter; and I am made still happier by the conviction that all that is important in that joyful experience will, after a little farther agitation (an agitation constantly diminishing not as to strength, perhaps, but as to the length of its cycles), become your permanent possession. It was not any confidence in your own love to Christ, but a confidence in the unmeasurableness of God's love, and of Christ's all-sufficiency for impotent humanity, and thus for a little "mote" like yourself, that made you so happy. Under your former views you always supposed that such revelations could not be made to you, except on a condition of personal attainment—some voluntary self-sacrifice. You began with a violent assault upon self (such, at least, was your theory), expecting by a most laborious process, if even possible at that, to get yourself thawed into some flexibility. But under a different instruction you have learned that the real condition of vitality, the whole secret of it lies in a passive receptivity; that the sun in infinite volume is already shining on you, and around you, and will shine in you with his divinest rays, if you will but open your senses to admit him.

Now, will you believe it, you have only to get that doctrine (of passive receptivity) firmly settled in your *understanding*, to have all that was important in your late happy experience, a permanent thing. For the truth is, that doctrine, though it may seem otherwise, is still rather a nebulosity in your heavens. It is only a little sunny fringe on the edge of the cloud which has awakened you to transport; but after a little more agitation the clouds will be dispersed forever, or become about as infrequent and transient as the sunshine has hitherto been, and then your peace will be as a river, and joy will be the law of your being. Still dissatisfied with yourself, and all the more, perhaps, from finding how little permanent improvement your late happy experience has wrought, the struggle with self will be renewed with even a stronger tendency, it may be, to a self-righteous confidence than you felt before, for it will appear but reasonable that, having received such a special blessing, your future progress in joy will depend on a special improvement; and when you find yourself doing no more than you have done hitherto, and not a whit better in yourself for all you have received, your agitation or your dejection may, for a while, be deeper than ever. I am describing an experience which may be possible. It is possible also, however, and I trust it may prove to be the fact, that you have already got beyond it. At any rate, it can last but a little while. The principle of passive receptivity has been inaugurated; the incorruptible seed has been deeply rooted. Every farther agitation by these trials of heart and conscience, to which you have so long been subject, will make it strike still deeper, and after a little farther discipline of sorrow, your sun of joy will rise and shine to God's glory, with scarcely a cloud, forever. Do not ask for any other *fruit* than this. It is Inspiration which tells us that the fruit of the Spirit is love, joy, peace; and our Saviour says that the end of all His instructions is, "that your joy may be full."

Let this doctrine, then, of doing nothing but receiving, which experience as well as Scripture shows us to be the real Gospel, be recommended to you still farther by its being the only doctrine which can produce the fruit that God desires. * * * * * I wish I knew how to rectify your mind fully on the subject of sanctification. The only danger of your steadfastness in the doctrine of passive receptivity, upon which I know your final faithfulness depends, arises from the restlessness of your mind upon the subject of sanctification,—and that arises from your still imperfect conceptions not of the nature of sanctification, in which I think you are just right, but of the method by which we reach and grow in it. I wish you could trust Christ's all-sufficiency here,—His love, and wisdom, and power, and faithfulness, just as you trust Him for justification. Just leave the matter in His hands, persuaded that all your regrets for being no better, and all your trying by such regrets, or any active efforts to mend yourself will but complicate your difficulties. My dear child, I promise you—speaking from a thorough experience—that if you will learn to commit all your interests into Christ's hands with the same simplicity which you would feel in trusting them to the dearest earthly friend, the true theory and secret of overcoming the world and self will gradually develop itself. He asks nothing of you but to continue presenting your sincere petitions to Him, whatever your frame may be, and then to trust Him to fulfill them. You have nothing else to do in the matter, and when you come really to do nothing else, matters will become wonderfully clear. It is your faith that He wants and nothing besides. That is the only form in which, for a time, He would have you manifest your love. When you have learned to do that well, He will give you the ability, through that faith, to manifest it in other ways. * * * * * I am full of earnestness to have you read Robertson's sermons. I have a number of sets purchased for distribution, one of which I shall express to you to-day. I am sure they will give you great delight. Never did you read such exquisite portraitures of the human heart. They rank in my mind with the choicest gems of art. Byron himself had not more of artistic beauty. Here are truths and modes of presenting them, which will make you forget your individual sorrows in a sense of the glorious universe of which you are a part. He sometimes speaks more from his feelings than from his understanding, which betrays him occasionally into an error of expression, which one can hardly think was his real sentiment, and there is by no means a full representation of many important truths; but what wondrous insight he shows into the *spirit* of the Christian revelation: and what a man for variety in a sermon! See the one on the healing of Jairus' daughter,—see them all in fact.

V.

I WISH I could tell you how great was the benefit which I received from your words of kindness to myself, and much more from the report which you give of your own inward relations to the Friend whose love to us gives our own love to each other so much of its significance. I am learning, with you, to think infinitely more of Him than of myself. I am willing to fail if He drops me. He cannot do wrong. I have no faithfulness but what is inspired by my belief in His. I wish no success, not even spiritual, but such as will make me reflect His radiance. I am overwhelmed with horror when I fall into a legal state, as I do occasionally for a small moment,—but from the very grave His voice raises me. That voice never rebukes, except as the " Lovest thou me " rebuked Peter. It never commands, but in a manner which implies that even failure to fulfill will but make me the object of his deeper sympathy. "Only trust me—trust me at the worst. All shall be well at last." This is the word which penetrates to the marrow of selfishness and kills it.

Such, dear brother, is *our* Saviour. Last Sabbath, at the communion, which I administered to a poor congregation a few miles from the city, I had a real taste of the heavenly vintage—a sight of Canaan's goodly land, not beyond what I had hoped for, but quite equal to my hopes of what it might be in this life. I had a glimpse of the *fullness of Christ*, and together with that, I saw, as I scarcely ever saw before, the element of *freeness*, which makes the Gospel so appropriate to sinners, by which it was manifest that even I might get all its blessings for myself, and by preaching which, I might even be an instrument of good to others. Since that, a new view of the Gospel has been coming over me, and yet not new, but the old Gospel which gave me my first hope. The old doctrine of salvation by Grace alone, sovereign Grace, which makes eternal life and all its antecedents the simple gift of God, bestowed wholly for the sake of Christ, and received by faith alone.

I see, for example, with heavenly certainty, that what God demands of you and me, especially with reference to the honor of the Gospel, of which we are ministers, and the welfare of souls, so many of which are dependent on us, to say nothing of our own peace and progress, is nothing, really nothing at all, but to *give up* that tremendous effort which we are always making to be something in His sight—and to be so infinitely satisfied with Christ (*God's gift* to us), as to be incapable of a care about ourselves—though not, therefore, of a care for Him, or for His honor. For myself, dear brother, I feel that even sin—the strength of the temptations to which I never felt more pressingly than now—is utterly harmless, such a sense have I of — what shall I call it? God's truth in Christ

God's fidelity to the vilest—my first and only duty being to trust in Christ forever. This is the truth which has brought me light, the old Gospel indeed, but so stripped of encumbering wrappings which hindered its highest efficacy, that I feel as if I had emerged from the gray dawn in which I have often only tremblingly rejoiced, into the glowing daylight of full deliverance.

Christ has redeemed us from the Law, and thus does he redeem us from sin, and death, and hell. Our immortal life, our eternal amaranthine crown, are just as secure as if we had been laboring for them for ten thousand years. This, just this, nothing less than this is the news, the glad tidings of great joy which the Gospel has brought to us. We just so far deny the Lord that bought us as we do not enter into it continually, and maintain as free a communion with God, as if we were conscious of a perfect personal righteousness; if we do not daily ask Him for whatever we want—for temporal things, with a child's submission to the parent's wisdom, and for whatever concerns our salvation, and the salvation of others, without a doubt of receiving, in due season, above our thoughts.

I have faith to believe that light and blessedness and glory will come out of all my past miseries, and whether the perfect day shall shine on earth or not, is a matter, personally, of little consequence. I have no preference of one way of doing God's will to another. I want only the consciousness of doing the work to which God has appointed me, and for which He has fitted me, to make me the happiest of all creatures; though long and earnestly have I hoped that God would enable me yet to do something more than I have ever done for others, that by some outward fruit it might be made apparent that my life, in which has been such waywardness, has, nevertheless, been directed and overruled by Him.

Of one thing I am sure : our whole sanctification and fruitfulness proceeds from nothing else but that spirit of love and gratitude which grows out of the apprehension of the perfection of Christ as a Saviour, and that we have nothing to do, if we would attain the highest perfection as Christians, and the highest success as Ministers of the Word, but to make nothing of ourselves—as well of our sanctification as of our sins; to think of nothing, to hope for nothing, to preach nothing, but the all-sufficiency of Christ.

For some years, as you may have surmised, I inclined to a more philosophical, or less simple interpretation of the method of salvation, making everything to depend indeed on faith, but viewing faith itself as something else than the mere hand which receives salvation. But I feel now, glory to God, that our salvation is perfectly accomplished, and that we have nothing to do but to *receive*—resting absolutely upon the merits and power and love of our Redeemer. The vision of Jesus ! pray for it continually. This is what gives the death-blow to sin—takes the life out of it, by a very simple process. By simply " looking " at the great Sacrifice, looking at it under all its aspect, suntil our sinning nature has absorbed the whole of its manifold significance. * * * * K—— left us this morning with her husband and the children for their new home—like an army with banners, so full of joy and triumph, though the atmosphere was all in a snowy rage.

I am busily engaged in my studies, with abounding hope and enjoyment.

VI.

I HAVE had a time of great peace since you were here—not the deepest—but crumbs from the Lord's table are worth more to me than crowns or kingdoms. * * * * * I wish exceedingly that I could show you clearly, in reply to your inquiry, the grounds of my confidence. Certainly, if I were conscious that my life had not been one of endeavor to do right I should quail. But though conscious of the contrary, yet with what I now see of the depths of selfishness and deceit which have really mastered my good endeavor, I should quail as much, if it were not for the blessed revelation of God in Christ—a just God, but all His justice satisfied in the Atonement. In the face of the deepest self-condemnation, I feel myself *bound* to believe the Word of God, and the revelation of the all-sufficiency of Christ.

I have been convinced from the Scriptures, that just as certainly as it is God's will that we should be holy and glorify Him in our lives, it is His will also that we first believe in His Son, of which the main and almost the engrossing idea is, to express it in the language of Edwards, that "we should hide ourselves in the ample folds of Christ's righteousness." I have long since learned that continuance in the love of God is not assured by a life of holiness, and never was intended to be. It is assured by the work of Christ *for us;* and trusting in that work, or resting upon it, one may be just as certain of His love as if he were already in glory, " for whom He justifies them He also glorifies."

I am confident that I want holiness infinitely more than mere assurance, in proof of which it is sufficient to say that my ordinary prayer, which is anything but a form, is that God would manifest His paternal interest in me by making me the subject of discipline rather than of comfort. But I am entirely convinced at the same time that the way in which we commonly seek these things, making holiness the basis of assurance, instead of assurance the basis of holiness, is directly opposed to the wisdom of God in the plan of salvation. The Bible here is at variance with our best philosophies. God's condescension to poor, fallen, diseased man is greater than man can give Him credit for until compelled by extremities. The truth is, the most of our philosophies are intended as counterparts of Grace, or as checks to Antinomianism;

and very certainly faith is opposed to Antinomianism on the one hand as strongly as it is to legalism on the other, and about every difficulty we have may be classed under one or the other of these heads. But "as the law was not made for a righteous man," where the desire for holiness is supreme, no other check is needed.

Any restraint, or limitation, or qualification of the doctrine of Grace, where a soul is conscious of a sincere desire for holiness is from the devil. I have no doubt, my dear brother, that you are not only entitled by the free grant of the Gospel, but are also qualified by your personal experience and aspirations for the largest liberty; that it is God's special will that you should exercise it, and that it is not merely the influence of your former habits of unbelief, but the peculiar power and malice of Satan, with whose devices you are not fully acquainted, which prevents your enjoyment of this spiritual freedom. I suspect also, that your philosophy stands in the way of your faith in the most vitalizing doctrine of the Gospel; though I can easily understand how it may rather help your general faith in Christianity.

Does not Coleridge, with what dear Dr. Cox

might call "the magnific wilderness of his ratiocinations," stand between you and the sincere Word? He could not understand the idea of an "imputed righteousness," nor could Schleiermacher. Why? Because, with all their talk of religion being a life, they were much more interested in it as a science. For the latter, as for sundry other Germans, there is some excuse. They cannot maintain the claims of the Gospel against German philosophy, which seems to be their mission, without giving up a part of it. The part which they give up is the part which Paul, whose mission was not to philosophers but to men, and whose concern was wholly for the "life," is most strenuous to hold. I accept Olshausen's view of imputed righteousness as the very best that I know. It gave me more strength when I first read it than anything I had seen on the subject.

Let me quote from Olshausen on Romans iv. 3–5, "If faith turns away from its proper object, the Christ without us, as the ground, not the consequence, of redemption: and if the man only considers himself the object of the divine favor, because he discovers Christ in himself, and only as long as this is the case, then faith altogether loses its proper nature, and the man falls again under the law." * * * * * No language can describe the interest with which I have read Skinner's "Vinèt." I would direct you to certain parts of it, if I were not certain that if you once begin you cannot lay it down for anything else till you have finished it. He constantly quotes Newton's "Cardiphonia." * * * * * We are all well. Is it not wonderful how long we are generally permitted to say this, and how sad a proof of our depravity that we generally need a stroke of the rod to make us appreciate this and many other blessings? We talk here as though we intended spending the summer in Lenox. Do you expect to leave there? You must go where Providence opens the way, but I am afraid that without you we shall have to say of Lenox as Byron said of Greece, to us at least it will be *living* Lenox no more. For myself, I expect the cloister life of Charles V. will be there repeated; but that too has its charms. Will such pleasant hours as we have spent together ever come again? Yes, far pleasanter. We are God's, and He will do for us far above our low, distrustful thoughts. "We are Christ's, and Christ is God's." What infinite joy is before us in the world of unclouded Light and Love!

VII.

As we are about to separate for a long time I am glad I have something definite to say to you—a very distinct direction to give you, by following which you will, in due time, reach the New Jerusalem, our happy Home, towards which we have so long been marching together, and where we shall find our everlasting rest. And for this particular stage of your earthly journeyings which you are now about to undertake, may you be attended by a guard unseen, a ministry of angels, and by their care be brought safely to the end.

My direction to you in your spiritual march is, to be patient, trustful, and joyfully expectant. Love asks for nothing but confidence. I do not know whether I clearly understand your ideas of "rejoicing with trembling;" but I think all the difference between us is that you hold that two and two make four. I insist that three and one make four! I could do nothing unless I *began* with joy—with an assurance of victory. The key-note of the New Testament exhortations certainly is not fear. Rejoicing and trusting in the Lord forever, and being sure that He will hear you in all that you ask Him, and never wavering in your confidence—seem to me as well the natural effect of evangelical truth as the substance of apostolic exhortation.

There are two ways by which the soul's activity may be stimulated, which are just the antipodes of each other—the certainty of the object sought, and its uncertainty; its certainty arising from the infallibility of the Saviour's love, and its uncertainty arising from the fallibility of ours. Before Christians can make any progress, their spiritual activity must cease to be damped by any such uncertainty. In resting upon Christ alone as their law-fulfiller, they must see that they are virtually obeying the whole commandment of the Gospel; for in no other way can love be generated.

Why did our Saviour address the fears of His disciples so little, their hopes so almost wholly? Why instead of so addressing them that their "joy might be full," did he not aim to burden them with care and responsibility? Was not His special design generally—in connection with giving instruction—to encourage and strengthen the weak and dejected? The idea that our Lord had it in His mind, to lay down tests and conditions which should throw the slightest uncertainty on the future prospects of His disciples whom He addressed, is so incongruous with the sympathetic movements of His soul, as in every way manifested, that it refutes itself.

Who were the persons, what was their quality, from whom He could not separate until he had made them as certain as He then could make them of the glory which should succeed their temporary darkness? (See those sublime words of tender love: John x. 14, and chapters following.) Upon the first trial all forsook Him, and one of them, who was thought to love Him most, with oaths and curses denied Him. Can you conceive then that He should have made the glory which He was promising them conditional upon a *character* which they had yet to attain, and which possibly they might never reach? How entirely would such a conception, had there been any foundation for it in their minds, have withered all the consolation of the address, and frustrated its chief design.

Take your stand with those disciples. Listen

with them to those comforting words of the Redeemer—He who has come in the likeness of your own sinful flesh, that He might make His soul an expiatory offering for all your sin past and future, in that respect, by that one offering "perfecting you forever;" and then, before returning to His Father, and your Father, to His heaven and your heaven, though His soul is exceedingly sorrowful in prospect of the sufferings before Him, as the burden of His last address to you, to guard you in every conceivable way against discouragement, present or future, hear Him saying, "Let not your heart be troubled; though I am going away, it is to receive the reward of my sufferings—a reward of which, in due season, you shall be a partaker with me; I go to fulfill an office for you in my state of glory, without which my sufferings for you would be to no purpose; I go to prepare a place for you in my Father's house, from which I will soon return to take you to myself, that where I am there you may be also, never more to be separated. And meanwhile our separation shall be only outward—I will not leave you comfortless; in a way of which you shall soon have an experience, I will manifest myself to you. I cannot, indeed, promise you an exemption from worldly trials; and that you may not be offended when they come, I feel it necessary to impress it upon you that from such trials, and manifold too, there can be no discharge. *Only be of good cheer;* all power is committed to me in heaven and on earth, and be assured that no trial shall be permitted but that—with faith in me—may be easily borne, and shall issue in a deep and abiding peace." Tell me, is not this the only true presentation of Christ, of His character, and His relations to our fallen humanity? Is not this the *glad tidings?* Depend upon it, my dear friend, and this is my farewell word, "long-suffering with *joyfulness*" is the way by which you will soon emerge from the chrysalis state into a new world in which your sun will never be clouded. This is the wing which will bear you upward into the spiritual empyrean.

To help your upward flight I send you Roundell Palmer's "Book of Praise," to which you may have seen some references in the journals; singular from the position of its compiler, he being no less a person than Queen Victoria's Solicitor or Attorney General, and its intrinsic merit is considerable. It is such at least that I had to read it straight through without omitting one of its four hundred hymns, and with precious effect upon my mind. It is far from containing all the good hymns, but so far as I can judge it is a good selection, from their having an equal reference to spiritual and poetical merit. I inclose a list of some which I liked much. See Charlotte Elliot's in particular. I will venture to send you also "Meditations on the Last Days of Christ," by a German missionary, which I am reading with great delight.

I shall pray constantly that the Lord may direct and bless you in all your ways.

VIII.

ONCE in a while I write to you from an oasis in the desert, but just now I am trudging it over the sandy plain, which makes up much the larger part of the pilgrimage of life. But I am full of courage, for I am sure Canaan is not far off. If we can only maintain this assurance (with full confidence in our leader, which rely upon it is the main thing in this world which is ruled by the devil and unbelief), it matters very little by what way we reach our home, supposing of course the assurance to be of the right kind, and on the right basis.

With your struggle to believe, dear brother, your hoping against hope, I fully sympathize. I have had all the difficulties which you describe about appropriation of the promises of the Gospel --all those for example which arise from the long habit of listening to and appropriating (because deserving) the voice of condemnation, and all those which arise from a consciousness that sin still has a hold on my nature, and my will, and those which spring from what you call "the weariness of holding on." But does not this very trouble and anxiety which such developments occasion reveal the existence of a Divine seed, which, insignificant as it seems at present, is destined to triumph over all the obstructions of a naturally uncongenial soil? * * * * * The only thorough proof which we have of the truth of our religion, of its principles as revealed in God's Word, or of their life and reality in ourselves, is that which arises from the triumph of simple faith over every form and kind of opposition. Have not nearly all of our difficulties from the beginning arisen from an unwillingness to walk by faith, demanding sight instead? Thus, for example, in matters of doctrine, we demand that before believing the truth firmly it must be made somewhat plainer to our reason, instead of embracing it at once, heartily and entirely, moved simply by the infinite condescension of God in speaking to us at all. In matters of duty, we wait for a farther consciousness of inherent ability, before undertaking it, instead of depending wholly and simply upon God's promise that strength shall not be wanting. This, the former, is what I mean by sight, and you see how exactly opposed it is to the principle of faith. We cannot but desire sight; sight is heaven; the very end of all our struggles. But the only way to attain it is to *begin with faith*, and so to continue. In truly believing, or in receiving the truth upon God's testimony only, the reason of it becomes increasingly, though it may be gradually, apparent, and our faith being thus strengthened, we are enabled to go on still more simply. In like manner, as we undertake duty in dependence only upon God's promise to work in us, and for us, this strength is made perfect in our weakness—is the greater in proportion to that weakness. And by such experiences the principle or habit of faith is constantly increasing.

Christian progress depends wholly upon keeping up the life of faith, and that depends upon steadfastly resisting the demand for sight. This is sanctification which is perfect only when self is so far subdued that walking by faith has ceased to be a trial. * * * * The root of much of our perplexity as Christians, lies in not properly estimating the comparative power of the old man and the new, or of grace and sin; between which the disproportion is such for a long time, and indeed even to the end of life, that just in so far as we are in the habit of looking into ourselves for grounds of comfort, we must be subject to despondency. The main difference between a weak Christian and a strong one, is, that the latter by temptation, for there is no other way, (James i. 12), has been weaned from this habit entirely—has learned to live by faith wholly. He lives, yet not he but Christ liveth in him. There is always a two-fold process going on in the Christian, as there are two great mysteries, with which every regenerate soul, in order to its perfect development, must be made acquainted—the mystery of God's love, and that of its own sinfulness and misery; and it seems certain that the first can only be reached through the other.

The Israelites who felt most painfully the bite of the serpent, and who seemed to themselves most hopelessly wounded, were those, doubtless, who experienced most fully and sensibly the power of the remedy. But the trouble is we never can, in this life, get to the bottom of ourselves, so as to be saved from being bitten again. Often as we have been wounded, and often as we have been recovered, the same experience has to be gone over again, with, of course, constant modifications. Just as in the type, God did not remove the fiery serpents, or not all at once, but healing was to be found in the midst of them, by looking to the brazen serpent,—so the temptations and conflicts of sin never leave the believer, but in the midst of them, with the eye of faith fixed on the uplifted Son of God, he *lives*—he shall never perish. At the end of life's struggle we find, it may be, a complete personal victory, yet far from our grasp. It is only by a constant reliance upon Him who has gained the victory eternally for us, that we are kept from sinking. But there is one thing in which, if we are really sincere, we are always gaining—that is, in the firmness and tenacity of that reliance, and this exactly in proportion as we are losing confidence in the possibility of complacency in personal attainments. I could not endure my existence if I had not the hope of being able to do more and better for Christ, but I expect no gain to myself from it. In my personal consciousness I shall be still poor and miserable for anything I may yet be or do. It is only death that shall be real and eternal gain. Then, if not in the midst of the last struggle, yet in the state which immediately succeeds it I shall be conscious of an immortal victory. I believe that Christ will *give* it to me as firmly as I believe that He has *gained* it for me.

* * * I knew you would find a feast in Dr. Hopkins' "Moral Science." I incline strongly to his view and yours as to the ultimate motive—that it is the *good* rather than the *right*, and suppose that if I ever find rest at all in reference to this disputed question, it will be there. But generally of late I try to stave off great philosophical or psychological conclusions, lest they might warp my spiritual ex-

perience. As to your criticism of the first question in the catechism, that "enjoy God" should go before "glorifying Him," I suppose you only mean that, in the nature of things, we must enjoy God before we can fully glorify Him. Surely this is self-evident; but still God's glory, in distinction from our own good, must be the final end. In the next world we shall see that more clearly and feel it more instinctively than we can in this, where we are only in training for our high vocation. Let us pray for each other without ceasing, and, after a little more struggling here, may we enjoy together the rest above.

IX.

YOU will find my text in the following sentence of your last epistle: "I do not find my heart drawn closer and closer to Christ in that mystic but undoubted union for which I am ever yearning." This may be accounted for in part by your circumstances through the summer, of which you had previously spoken. Nevertheless, I am very glad that you have had so much pleasure—so much relief from the monotony of your usual life. God gave it to you in love as a means of physical recreation. It would indicate that autumnal maturity had arrived indeed, if you had found that the abundance of God's outward blessings had not a stronger tendency to withdraw your heart from Him, than to bind it to Him. Such blessings, for blessings they truly are, ought, indeed, to have the opposite effect, and in the autumn time, when it comes, they will doubtless have the opposite effect upon you. But if for the present and for some time to come these natural gifts of God should still have the effect to discover your treachery to the Giver, rather than your fidelity to Him, think it not strange, for even a Henry Martyn, as I well remember, has told us the same story.

Any Christian, any child of God, who seeks or expects worldly happiness out of a certain order will assuredly be disappointed. *First* seek the kingdom of God and His righteousness—the perfect reign of the love of God in the heart, and all other things shall be added; that is the order, and "first" there has the force of *only*. Seek only inward spiritual purity, taking it for granted that this will bring in its train whatever else is really good. This attained, the least earthly good will give you more earthly happiness than the greatest could without it; and there is no way of attaining it in its fullness, or, in any sufficient or satisfying measure but by persevering in seeking it only. Remember farther, that on the great principle in which I have taken such pains to establish you, the principle of a free justification, you cannot fail to be attaining it daily; and you may seek it to the end of life with ever-growing encouragement. The vexation arising from the strength of your natural desires will be constantly diminishing—not sensibly, perhaps, during short intervals of time, but very sensibly in greater intervals.

But let me now express my joy that you are still waiting for the realization of that "mystic union" (which according to my conception of it can hardly be called mystic), our common faith in which is the chief bond of our spiritual fellowship. Let me freshly assure you that I have no other conception of "Life." Be grateful even for the idea—much more for the promise of a relation to Himself, which I have not a doubt that the strongest and sweetest of our natural desires were given to us for the express purpose of foreshadowing—and which besides being in such clear analogy with nature, so perfectly corresponds to the dominating attribute with which Christ has invested Himself. To be filled with such an idea and such a promise—can you conceive of a higher favor to a human soul than this? But do you ever conceive that it is just this favor which makes our life on earth one protracted sigh? "We spend our years *as a sigh.*" So the Syriac version of the Old Testament (Tayler Lewis tells me), renders the phrase which we translate "as a tale that is told," in the ninetieth Psalm. It is the brightness of our hope which makes the present life such a shadow. The law which commands the ocean never to be still, is not more inexorable than that which must ever agitate a heart thus divinely wooed, until this idea has become a full-orbed reality, this promise an inalienable and conscious possession. * * * * * What makes our life a bondage, "a sigh," is, that the element of faith in the Saviour which is mixed with it, is so little. It saddens us chiefly to think what a dishonor such a life is to the Divine goodness, to the provisions of the Gospel, to the self-sacrificing love, and condescension, and faithfulness of the Good Shepherd. Why should we be so anxious, and unsettled, and distrustful, and joyless when such a Friend has died for us, lives for us, and is ever, if there is any truth in the Gospel, engaged to give efficacy to our prayers, and reality to our hopes? How can we be so heartless, when wooed by such importunity of self-devoting love? It is found in experience, that a little ingenuous confidence is not enough to break our bondage; but a little added to that, and a little more to that, will at last do it. Suppose Christ should reveal Himself personally to you and should say to you, "My little one" (the name, you know, which he gives to the least and weakest of His people), "my little one, so unlovely and unworthy in your own eyes, you are most precious in mine. I love you with a love which has no dependence upon your character, but rather has been excited by your utter helplessness, your poverty, your meanness, your weakness, your troubles and dangers, your bondage and misery, of which you are so sensible; these are your recommendations; these are the bonds by which you will for ever hold me. Henceforth you have nothing to do but to give me your confidence; and that I ask, not because any deficiency in it will turn my heart away from you, but only for your own sake. I want "your joy to be full." My love is free, and pure, and disinterested. It cannot be changed, but only be made more resolute, by your infirmities and dangers; though, to your own consciousness, until your faith is recovered, it must, of course, always appear otherwise.

But your salvation cannot fail. My honor is engaged for it. I have betrothed you to myself for ever, and there is nothing which my love can do for you, for which you may not at once command it. Begin the trial of it immediately; cast all your care upon me, and when the enemy appears, let it be a powerful worldly affection, a strong inducement to rest in the creature instead of going out to seek your rest and happiness in me; or, let it be a sense of coldness, and a want of confidence, which you think must provoke my displeasure, let it take what form it may, just come to me, and if you cannot speak for your confusion, just say in sobs and sighs, 'O my Jesus, my Jesus, my Jesus! Thou seest my misery, Thou knowest I cannot conquer this temptation.' Yet, Thou knowest too, how I desire to conquer it, and Thou hast told me never to doubt either Thy power or Thy love. Allured by Thy promises of certain victory in every conflict, I have cast away my own strength, and now trust entirely in Thine. And wilt Thou deceive me? Never, never! "Though Thou slay me, I will trust Thee!"

You tell me, perhaps, that Christ has not yet revealed Himself to you in the manner described. Let it be so. But has He not thus revealed Himself to humanity, to our nature? Is not this the exact significance of the Gospel Revelation, taking it as a whole? Is not this just what is meant by the height and depth, the length and breadth, of the love of Christ, which passeth knowledge? And is He not thus revealed generally, in order that any one who will, any one who is athirst for such a Saviour, and such a salvation, may make a personal appropriation of Him, and of it? and just as minute and particular an appropriation as he pleases to make—too particular it cannot be. And moreover, is not this just the view of Christ which has always allured you, especially within a few months past? Is not this the very relation to Him which you are trying to realize? Can anything satisfy you but to have it perfected? Would it not thrill you with joy to know assuredly that you were right on the way to it—that it was just before you? Then hear the voice of Jesus saying, "Be not afraid, only believe. In a little while I will come. I will not tarry."

Until now you have given Him your confidence, perhaps only in a faint and general manner; but having learned from your past experience that everything depends on the thoroughness of that act, you are now trying to confide in Him fully. Do you not see at once that a confidence produced by a personal revelation, or by a discernment of His particular affection for you would be a very poor act on your part, a very poor test of the state of your heart toward Him? The true and only foundation of confidence in Christ is the record which is given in the Scriptures of His life and character, of His relations to God and His relations to humanity, and the motive to confidence, and to a personal appropriating faith, is the desire of the soul for just such a Saviour and such a salvation—that deep and everlasting want which only such a Saviour can relieve.

It is certainly true that the faith inspired by the general revelation is infinitely vivified by the personal. But still, the general revelation is the foundation; and it is only by suspending the whole weight of the soul's cares, desires and hopes on that revelation, and in proportion as we do so, that we can reach anything special or personal.

And now, my dear child, I think you must see just where you are, and just what you have to do. Desire the personal expression as strongly as you please; thirst for it as for the water of life, for it is so; and be perfectly sure you shall obtain it; only remember that the way to it, to its first, and to every other degree of it, is by faith in the yet unseen. Rejoice that your dear Lord gives you the opportunity of showing how much you can trust Him. Say to Him boldly, "I am now so certain of Thy free and unmeasurable love that I will henceforth ask for no expression from Thee but what is necessary to Thine own glory; but this I must have—I must serve Thee—Thou only art worthy! Whatever is necessary to break in pieces this selfish heart, and to create an entirely new heart within me, a heart in which Thou shalt entirely reign, that is all I want. If it is necessary for a farther discovery of the root of evil in me, that Thou shouldst withhold a little longer the tokens of Thy special regard, behold my submission. Only let me have the privilege of calling Thee mine, until such time as Thou pleasest to give my hand, now outstretched in darkness, that firm grasp which shall make it sure forever."

SECTION II.

GROWTH IN GRACE,

PROMOTED IN THE SOUL THROUGH THE MINISTRY OF TRIAL.

"THAT the trial of your faith being much more precious than gold that perisheth, though it be tried with fire, might be found unto praise, and honor and glory at the appearing of Jesus Christ."—I Peter i. 7.

* * * * * No one can know the depths of grace, until he has experienced the depths of mortal sorrow. * * * * * Can you not see why it is that in answer to our most earnest and persistent prayers, it often happens that our Lord's love for us is expressed more by rebuke than by those special manifestations for which we pray? This is the way He fulfills His promises to those whom He loves. By temporal sorrows He shatters their earthly hopes that they may hope in Him alone. By spiritual trials He reveals the strength and depth of their corruption that they may know the power of His forgiving and sanctifying love. By "manifold temptations" He tries their faith in His love, and in His promise.

"Blessed is the man that endureth temptation, for when he is tried he shall receive the crown of life which the Lord hath promised to them that love Him." In proportion to your fidelity in enduring temptation you will find your faith growing into assurance, the promise becoming a possession, the conflict culminating in the crown.

SECTION II.

GROWTH IN GRACE,

PROMOTED IN THE SOUL THROUGH THE MINISTRY OF TRIAL.

I.

THERE was a passage in your last letter which has been ever since as "a sword in my bones," but which, though suffering so much by silence, I have not, till now, found any time to answer. The passage was this: "I do believe that the Law, the hard schoolmaster, has a tyrant's power over my heart, and I fear that I never shall escape from it. I feel that the phrase 'under conviction' expresses my state better than any other; but what a humiliating confession, after having for years professed to be a believer in Christ."

I had no time, in writing the letter to which this was an answer, to do any justice to the nature and designs of the operations of the Law upon the souls of the regenerate. It is a common idea that after a person has been really regenerated the Law has very little to do with him as a schoolmaster; and I fear that this is generally too true. But the reason is very different from the one you imagine. It is so, because people are so generally satisfied, through the power of self-love, with the hope of ultimate salvation—because they have not any strong desire for sanctification. It is quite otherwise with those who have an elevated Christian ideal, or a peculiar spiritual sensitiveness. Such persons have often to suffer long from the operation of the Law, simply as a schoolmaster; but it is just as certain as the truth of God, or as the operation of any natural law, that if this work is not arrested it must issue in an extraordinary measure of sanctification. What often arrests it in persons of unusual susceptibility for spiritual ideas and attainments, is the want of thorough evangelical instruction and encouragement. For the want of this they often diverge into some delusive form of spirituality.

How sure I am, taught by an infallible instinct, that in the natural course of your experience, if you can be well sustained by the right kind of sympathy and counsel, you cannot fail to attain a high degree of Christian confidence and spiritual illumination. The growing sense which you have of your own corruption and helplessness (which is the work of the Law), which makes your case appear to yourself so specially hopeless, fills me with confidence that you are going to experience in a peculiar manner the transforming power of the Gospel. My joy for you at present is, that you have learned what the *Gospel is*, and I do not believe you are going to be moved from it, nor from the hope which it inspires. See in Col. I. 22–23, how the Apostle connects this holding on to the hope of the Gospel with sanctification. Let me show what makes this so difficult. * * * * Regeneration does not arrest or suspend the operation of the Law, but it puts us in possession of a principle by which we are made able to bear it. Now, if we could only take the Law and Grace together, (which is our great comprehensive duty), holding with equal strength and pertinacity to both of them, not suffering the repose given by the latter to slacken the fiery operation of the first, nor the fiery work of the first to impair at all the confidence inspired by the other, we should soon attain assur-

4

ance and a consciousness of progressive sanctification. In other words we should soon be "rooted and grounded." But the work of the enemy when he cannot choke or check our aspirations for spiritual freedom by worldly hopes and promises,—when he cannot prevent the Law from disturbing and agitating us, is to destroy the hope and confidence (as to the final result) which the Gospel produces, and which is indispensable to the right operation of the other.

It will be a great help to you if you can only learn to discriminate between the work of God and the work of Satan in your present trial, for both are concerned in it,—the former, as your physician, who means only your health, though He has to prescribe the most disagreeable regimen and keep you under it (the convictions of the law); the latter as your enemy, who tries to persuade you, by very plausible reasons no doubt, that because your medicine does not immediately heal you, but rather makes you worse (for you seem to yourself at present to be growing worse rather than better), it is entirely inefficacious, and that you never will be any better. To stifle your hope from God's promise, to make it feeble and inoperative in prayer, to keep you in constant bondage to an evil conscience, that, my dear brother, is only the work of your adversary. God, you may be sure, has nothing to do with that.

Remember, there is no way of meeting the suggestions of your enemy but as our Saviour met them—from the Word of God. If you reason about them, separated from the Word, you are overwhelmed at once. O, how I long to see you established! * * * * * And now this is all that I have to say at present as to the nature of the blessing which is to grow out of your present trial. It is not sanctification in the highest sense, which can only be reached through separation by death from all the elements of temptation; but, a strong assurance that you are a child of God,—a strong sense of the love of God,—a complete change in your present habit of looking at yourself, depending on yourself, and judging of your state by what the Law reveals. I can assure you, you will soon realize a remarkable deliverance from the Law, and thus acquire a new power of living unto God. That faith which you now have, occasionally, will become a settled abiding and effectual principle of progress.

A distinctly new era is before you,—a bright era of love, and faith, and peace, for which your present experience—your long "conviction" has been *the* preparation. No other would have answered as well.

How can I feel any differently about you, when I have been through the very same experience myself, and when, through just such suffering of hope deferred as you are enduring now, it at length became plain to me that this very trial was God's method of sanctification! Certainly, I can say in view of the results, that nothing but the perpetual succession of trials through which my path in life has led, could have so demonstrated the Divine faithfulness. It has been by walking through the valley of humiliation that I have come into the consciousness of an eternal inheritance which I should have failed to reach in any other way. * * * I have only a moment more in which to give you my blessing. May the Lord be with you, giving you every blessing which you need, and of trials only such as you are able to bear, and in bearing which you will reach your highest end.

II.

I AM always overflowing with thoughts for you, but cannot always write. I have longed especially to say something more to you if I might, to encourage you in bearing your present spiritual trials. I know so well by experience the nature and bitterness of these trials, together with what you but partially know—the real reason and meaning of of them in God's plan—all that they portend and precede, that I ought to be able to say something for your help and encouragement.

(If the simple object of the Gospel were to give us comfort, or to make us perfectly happy at once, these self-revelations which bring so much humiliation and distress would not be needful.) But then there would be no chance for a thorough purification. And what is the real meaning of these trials? They are a part of God's plan for our sanctification. They are the beginning of our glorification—the essential means of it. They are the plucking up of the weeds which hinder the growth of the good seed. So far from being the expression of God's anger on account of remaining sin, they express His unchanging purpose to make us holy. He sees us in our folly still cleaving to the world, but yet with some sincere desire towards Him. He is determined that the desire shall not be disappointed, and, therefore, that the folly shall be utterly purged out; not a particle of it shall remain. It is sometimes a very long work, but not necessarily so, and it is always a sure one.

To a little child, the conduct of the husbandman in putting his ploughshare through a field of showy wild flowers, leaving in their place nothing but ugly furrows, would be anything but pleasing. It would give but little relief to see him throwing a small seed into the furrows too insignificant to be noticed, and then burying it entirely out of sight by the rude operation of the harrow. And yet, if the husbandman were his father, and should tell him that out of this destruction should spring up, in a little while, a world of far higher fertility and beauty, he might be reconciled to wait that "little while," by faith in the paternal promise.

Through me the Father tells you that the very thing you desire, but glorious as to measure and quality beyond any conception of it you can now form, will in a little while be yours.

Trial continues to reveal your bondage to self-love, is the burden of your complaint. There are two ways in which this experience may affect you painfully: First, by wounding your pride, and secondly, by giving an advantage to unbelief, renewing your doubts as to the efficacy of the Gospel in which you have trusted for a cure. The Divine reason why you are yet exercised in this painful way, is that the evil to be cured is not sufficiently probed. (Judge for yourself how far the pain you suffer from these failures arises from pride, from the laceration of self-esteem, from the sensitiveness of the diseased part—how far a different treatment would have rather tended to heighten your self-estimation, and to hide or cover over your weakness, than to demonstrate that it had been mortified.) This trying or probing work is going on in all the subjects of redemption; but with this difference as to its effect, that at first it scarcely does anything else but vex, and wound, and discover the power of our self-regard. But as it proceeds that effect becomes less and less. We are willing it should be so; we are humbled, but hardly dissatisfied. Since the evil is there, let it come out. There is nothing we are so much afraid of as spiritual self-exaltation—nothing we so much desire as to be thoroughly humbled. We still dread trial, and are most sensitive of failure; but there is this consolation in it, at the worst, that it does tend to the mortification and to the destruction of our pride and self-esteem, which we desire above all things, even when we are suffering the most. At last, when we become so much set upon the destruction of this principle that we rather invite the probe than fear it, and are entirely patient under its operation, then, when we are so well fortified against the evils which, in an earlier stage of our trial, might arise from spiritual victory and triumph, through the undiscovered subtlety of self-love, then the battle turns, and we go upward as rapidly as before we seemed to be going downward.

It is a great point gained when we have learned to believe that our spiritual trials are *necessary*, not *arbitrary*. These trials, arising from the growing knowledge of our selfishness, pride, and inconstancy, are the indirect means by which God's promises are fulfilled to us. It is not the *direct* effect of trial to sanctify us,—it sanctifies us only by leading us to Christ. This is the design of all our inward griefs and difficulties—to make us turn our eyes to the promises of God, and find in Christ the power which we have tried in vain to find in ourselves. It is astonishing what an amount of trouble we can endure before we are willing to give up self and find our all in God—how long we can be satisfied with partial reliefs; and, oh! what an amazing power of deceit there must be in sin which can so manage as to keep us through a great part of our lives resisting God's designs of love. * * * In supporting and carrying us through this conflict there is no one agency so indispensable as prayer. This, my dear friend, is the weapon with which you will overcome both the world and the devil. What you said in your letter about your incapacity for direct, warm-hearted prayer must be wholly altered, and will be, in the hour of trial. It is by such prayer only that we can overcome. * * * It is one thing to have the heart excited by a glorious prospect, while the difficulties connected with its realization are kept out of sight, and a very different thing to have the heart so fixed upon its attainment that in full view of all trials, of every kind, it still cleaves firmly to its object. When the Israelites were delivered from their bondage in Egypt, with the promise of the bright land for their inheritance, they made nothing of the intervening toils and dangers. They sang on the farther shore of the Red Sea as if the land were already possessed. But the fallacy of this calculation soon became a matter of painful conviction. They were not steadfast in the covenant; when they were tried they murmured.

I should not be your friend if I allowed you to think that through any other way than the one of conflict you could reach the bright ideal either of Christian privilege or Christian character. Does not our Lord always thus premonish his disciples? Do not His apostles the same? While the spiritual desire, or taste, or hope, or passion by which the sinful tendency might be regulated is not matured or established enough to do its work there must be conflict. Hence our Christian life is a *fight*, the good fight of faith, and in the earlier stages of it there is much danger as well as trial. But after a while we become grounded and settled. As the things of faith become near and living to us, the world loses it gloss and self yields. Prayer, in which we once had much difficulty, becomes our most delightful exercise; and at length we realize that blessed friendship with God which is the beginning of heaven.

Fight then, my dear friend, on your knees, with patience, for the work requires time; with faith, for God is in every trial—the loving God who, after you have been tried for a while, will stablish, strengthen, and settle you. Depending on His grace in Christ, you will triumph over all enemies within and without.

III.

NIGHT and day do I carry you in my thoughts and in my prayers, and there without a moment's weariness it shall be one of the most sacred privileges of my life to keep you, until in the embrace of the Chief Shepherd you have found a perfect rest. There I know indeed you are at this moment; it is only the consciousness of being there that is wanting, and that I am sure you will soon attain.

How well do I know that the aches and pains hardest to bear, arise from the predominence, which often seems almost hopeless, of the selfish element, and involves an almost unceasing self-condemnation. What, my dear child, is your heart-felt want? You told me you "wanted a thousand and one things." I thought, however, that you laid a special emphasis on the *one*, and I presume you would feel yourself no loser if you could secure the one, though you had to drop the thousand. First, to express it negatively, is it not to get rid of a selfish heart? Do you not find this to be your perpetual burden? God has made the world for your enjoyment, and given you a very large capacity for its pleasures, and yet you cannot enjoy it without bitterness to your conscience. You find that worldly enjoyment, even the most innocent in itself, is so apt to feed this moral distemper (inordinate self-love), that it is only by the utmost carefulness that you can prevent what has been given so freely for your happiness from becoming a snare and a pit-fall—and thus as to *natural* enjoyment, your life is very much of a bondage. You then try to regulate the matter by your *religious* exercises, but the fiend pursues you still. You find selfishness to be (generally perhaps), the predominating element in your prayers. What you pray for has such an almost exclusive reference to your own safety, honor, benefit—to your selfish though religious wants, that you have but little freedom in asking, and little hope in immediately or speedily obtaining. From the same cause, in reading the Scriptures, even the tenderest expressions of the Saviour's love to His brethren, to His dear lambs, to those for whom He gave His life, even the most glorious assurances of present and constant victory over all enemies—all that you can hope in regard to these is that some day or other you *may* experience their full significance. * * * * * To get rid of a selfish heart, which makes life a bondage—this is what you want; and the only way to be rid of this, is to have the heart filled with a new affection. Then will you have the long-desired rest, when you shall so feel the drawings of Christ that if you love anything else it will be for His sake—when He shall be your conscious all. This, and nothing else, you feel can be *Redemption* for you. That you shall reach this state, and far more abundantly than I have described it, I am just as certain as I am of the love and faithfulness of the Good Shepherd. Hitherto the union between your soul and Christ has been (to your own consciousness), mainly a legal union. You have followed Him chiefly from a sense of duty—from a fear of evil, and from a hope of final salvation. Your union with Him has been practically like that of a servant to a master; a good master indeed, who pardoned your faults, and occasionally smiled upon your efforts, provided you did the best you could. But, you have been habitually mourning over your own unworthiness, instead of rejoicing in the confidence of possessing His favor. And you see at length that thus it must always be, unless the relation, which according to the New Testament is of an entirely different character, becomes all that it is declared to be to your own consciousness. Through the trial which leads to this joy—this freedom, you are now passing. It is not more certain that day shall succeed the dawn, or the dawn the darkness, than that you, holding fast the truths you have heard, and patiently waiting for the fulfillment of Christ's promises, shall experience *fully* the redemption for which such a price has been paid. There are many reasons why it should come so gradually, but chiefly the danger of giving some advantage to self by a premature liberation. It comes gradually as every great conquest comes; but when everything has been prepared by a thorough self-mortification there will be a revelation of love and power. I do not see how any can ever know the power of the love of Christ, unless they have first been made to know thoroughly the depth of their own worthlessness, nor how the conviction of this can ever be produced but by long-continued failures in an effort to redeem themselves.

But guard against the idea that the revelation of Christ's love is withheld because of your present unworthiness, or from your failure to meet certain conditions upon which it depends. Those conditions are wrought in us—and He is all the while working them in you while you are expecting and praying for redemption on the basis of Christ's love, work and promises. Let nothing move you from that ground. Here you will find the adversary particularly active and fertile. But remember there can be no middle ground between works and faith. Let it be the effect of all your trials and disappointments only to fix you more firmly on the latter, for that is the main design of them.

Always look upon Christ as loving you already just as much as He ever will love you. If you fail, or seem to fail, in your returns to Him which you will always be trying to make, regard not such failures as affecting in the least His relation to you as the Good Shepherd, but rather as giving you a new claim upon His pity. He will find means in the end to make strength come out of weakness, and when all hope from works is entirely destroyed, you will find that power in faith, of which you have heard so much and realized so little.

Meanwhile my great concern is to prevent your mind from morbidly preying on itself, of which I am sure you are in much danger. Against this, one of the best remedies is reading good books—books which give large views of the Christian life, in distinction from the narrow, into which, actuated strongly by a single idea, we are liable to fall. As the first want of the body is good food, so truth is the first condition of a vigorous spiritual life. To meet this want I send you Stier's "Words of the Lord Jesus"—the first of six volumes. Try it, and report. Begin with the Sermon on the Mount, which, after reading this exposition of it, you will say you never comprehended before. You will find no difficulty from its criticisms on the original. It flows on as freely as a sermon; but it is sometimes so rich in its references that you are in danger of losing the thread, and it is a little obscure to an English reader not familiar with the peculiarities of the German mind. But I think it is the richest commentary upon Christ's discourses I have ever read; and yet it is easy to see that the author has been guided to his views far more by his spiritual experience than by the sharpness of his faculties. You may keep it just as long as you please, as I have access to another. It will search you, but there is enough to comfort. He *perfectly* understands the Gospel as well as the Law.

Next to good books or converse with large-souled men, as a means of mental health, is work, which is the same as exercise to the body. Make something for yourself to do, especially in giving spiritual help to those who are more needy than yourself. The law of Christ's kingdom is "Give, and it shall be given to you; for with what measure ye mete withal, it shall be measured to you again." The true method of securing a blessing to ourselves is to feel and labor for the benefit of other souls. Life is developed within us by the very exertion to promote it around us.

* * * I think I will send you also a volume of Archdeacon Manning's Sermons; though since they were published he has gone to Rome. On many accounts, and particularly on account of their high spirituality, and their very searching character, I have valued them for the last ten years more than almost any sermons in my library. They are also models of every intellectual excellence. Manning is one of the most inflexible advocates for holiness of the highest standard. Read, and report.

IV.

I HAVE not written to you, for the reason which the elder gave to the elect lady: "Having many things to write to you I could not write with paper and ink, but I trust shortly to see you face to face that your joy may be full."

A solemn joy is mine—a light from the eternal throne amidst a world of darkness. How can I express the various mingling colors of my soul? Sin and holiness are no longer words, but things. The forms breathe, they are alive. Oh, that I had the power of painting, instead of penning, the various states of mind, the deep and tender griefs, the holy and exalted joys, the struggles and surrenders, the straits and deliverances of the past few weeks! I have told you, I think, that my prayer for months has been that God would set up His tribunal in my bosom—that He would judge me now—that He would make me think of myself just as He does; that the work of the Law may be complete. The effect has not been death —or rather it has been death in order to life. God is love. Love's frown is the aspect which love assumes for its object's benefit, and as that is attained, love, and only love, appears. Of this I am now so entirely satisfied, that I no longer dread the Divine rebukes, but rather welcome them. I see the root of past unfaithfulness so clearly that it seems sometimes as though it would never spring up again to trouble me; and if I can be kept from the folly of thinking so, and feel every day that I am nothing but a mass of sin, I may do a little for Christ. Oh, to do something, before I die, for Jesus Christ! I am engaged with an interest which I never felt before in preaching the *Gospel*—particularly the Atonement, in its relations to spiritual life and holiness. You will think it strange, perhaps, when I tell you that one of my favorite points in preaching is God's end in the permission of evil. This has become a practical matter with me. Sin may be part of God's plan for making the universe more deeply holy. I can see now, how, through the Atonement, all my bondage to sin will be overruled, to give me stronger conceptions both of the Divine justice and grace—of the evil and hateful nature of sin, and of God's pure goodness, than I could have had in any other way. * * * The great mystery of the Christian's experience is, that often faith and prayer fail to give the mastery over the evils of his heart. He seems to depend only on the Divine faithfulness, and yet the enemy is not expelled. He perceives a difference, indeed, answering to the old promise of the expulsion of the Canaanites, "by little and little." But why by little and little, with such alternations of defeat, and the victory, perhaps, at last scarcely gained? His defect in sincerity does not solve the difficulty, for that is the enemy which he depends on God's faithfulness to extirpate.

I think I see the solution at length pretty clearly. A father who wishes to produce in his son the deepest abhorrence of vice and the most perfect love of virtue, would not so remove him from temptation, even if he could, as absolutely to secure him from falling. A virtue thus gained would hardly deserve the name. Nor, if he could foresee (as God does in virtue of the atonement), that the effect of his fall would be to give life and vigor and depth to the principle of virtue, would he put forth his whole power to prevent it, though not for worlds would he exert a direct agency in causing him to fall. I must add that this principle has given me a heart-satisfying insight into the deep mystery of moral evil as connected with the destiny of our race, and the history of the universe, and of the nature of the life of God in the soul. You will not wonder that, hearing lately a sermon undertaking to show that for all the Gospel can do, the redeemed will have occasion through all eternity to lament that they were sinners, "I withstood Peter to the face," thinking that "he was to be blamed" for so limiting the Almighty in his power to bring good out of evil! * * * * I have come to a pretty clear conclusion that there is a peculiarity in all genuine Christian experience which it takes a great while to learn, and which many, perhaps, never learn at all, the knowledge of which is very essential to our peace. It appears quite certain to me that God's way of bringing us to realize our ideas of holiness is very different from the way of our expectations. It seems indispensable to the purging of our souls from pride, and other spiritual uncleannesses, that we should sometimes be left apparently very much to ourselves without the *consciousness* of God's support, or any constraining spiritual power. "These many years have I led you in the wilderness, to humble and prove you, that ye may know what is in your heart," or "whether," left to yourselves, "ye would obey my commandments or not." Let us not lose sight of the conclusion, "that I might do you good in your latter end."

Certainly there is no avoiding a life-long struggle with corruption. But as God has promised us the victory in the struggle, it seems difficult to reconcile the promise with the ordinarily depressed condition of those who, in the judgment of charity, we nevertheless recognize as Christians. The whole difficulty arises from not giving sufficient latitude to the promise—a latitude required by the nature and design of the conflict. As the struggle is to be life-long, if support enough be given to endure it to the end, and the victory be won at last, the promise is fulfilled—though in the result of each particular struggle there may be more matter for shame than for exultation. The power of the Spirit in us is not to be measured by our present success—few can testify to that as the rule in their spiritual history—but by our persevering hope when success seemed scarcely possible; by our continuance in faith and prayer while victory seems far distant—the victory at least which we feel to be necessary to the insurance of our title to the crown. * * * * And yet let us guard against the perversion of this doctrine of gradual sanctification. While there is no doubt that it is a life-long work, how gradual it shall be depends very much upon the nature and strength of a person's desire for it. How easy to impute to its gradual character what arises from our unwillingness to be sanctified—that is, to seek all our satisfaction in God. "If ye through the Spirit (with what life ye have) do mortify the affections of nature, ye shall live." Do we not find our only life in the prospect of perfect holiness? Are we not becoming more and more unreconciled to sin?

Let us "stand fast in the Lord," dearly beloved; and this is to stand fast in the great principle that salvation is of God; not merely in the sense of His being the Author of the plan, but especially in the sense of His being the doer of the work.

V.

No letter I ever received from you has touched my spiritual sympathies more deeply than your last to me; and I cannot let another mail go without bearing to you at least a few words for your cheer—a poor word (cheer) to express the immeasurable consolation to which you are entitled. If your letters at present were anything but what they are—sad complaints of self, sustained in a good degree by hopes of a future deliverance—hopes founded not so much on anything yet experienced, as on the doctrine about Christ and Grace which you have learned, I should be entirely disappointed. You never wrote a letter to me the tone of which was more to my heart's desire than the last; but what shall I say of the contents, evincing how much you have yet to learn of your own heart, of the power of sin, and of the only method of overcoming it? You say you "cannot any lon ger burden (me) with these oft-repeated complaints," you "cannot keep coming with the same old, sad story, that you are really doing nothing but *holding on*," etc. The truth is, my dear child, you are *not* holding on—that is the "sad story" which these words convey to me, notwithstanding your after-affirmation to the contrary, to prevent my discouragement, which by the way was very unnecessary. If you knew how much I have suffered from the same causes which make your life (for the present) a monotone of sadness, you would never, never be prevented from writing to me by the idea that I could be wearied, or oppressed, or perplexed, or discouraged, by your spiritual complaints.

Very certainly, if it were directly revealed to me that in consequence of some constitutional weakness, or some spiritual malformation, your spiritual life would be one of perpetual cheerlessness, it would have no other effect but to give a life-long tension to my sympathy: I should be all the readier to stand by you to the bitter end. Do not think that I am in the slightest degree discouraged or even disappointed by the expressions quoted. I know too much of such a frame—how much more it springs from ignorance than from anything else —to have much concern about it. It shows the earnestness of your self-dissatisfaction, and of your desires for holiness. But it shows, also, how much you have yet to learn of your own weakness and of the all-sufficiency of Christ, if you suppose that you can ever attain a higher state of holiness in this life than that which is expressed by simply "holding on" to Him. How long it takes to learn the simplest truths, and how often, in our discouragement, we say, "what an idle thing is this faith!" We do, indeed, despise ourselves that for so long a time, we can show no other proof of being in Christ, or of Christ being in us, but the tenacity with which we hold to this faith. And it would be an idle faith, indeed, except for the condition of soul in which it is held—the condition of deep legal trial, or efforts for sanctification. It is the union of the two things which gives faith all its value.

You have nothing to do but to *hold on.* Your inward trials at present are the indications of life, of growth; they are the growing pains of spiritual adolescence. Do not look at yourself for any other purpose but to learn how weak you are, and to have a stronger argument for saying to Christ, "See how entirely I depend on Thy love and Thy work for me—and depend I will—how else can I do Thee any honor?" Just think of Him as conducting the work of grace in your heart as he conducts the growth of things in nature, which, with all pull-backs, is ever making progress. "How much more shall He clothe you—of little faith"—and in spite of its littleness.

I have just been reading the following sentence in a German book: "It is in the kingdom of God as it is in nature. In March, the green blades from the seeds, however unassuming they appear, have a greater *future* than the masses of snow by which they are still covered. Not at once does the spring sun obtain a victory over the snow and ice, but the gray masses of ice in the hollow ways do not stop the spring,—it is spring nevertheless. The sun becomes more and more powerful, and the winter becomes weaker and weaker;" not, observe, to your consciousness, it may be, at present, but be sure that God has nothing in the future for you but blessing, if you will dismiss every care but that of trusting Him, and doing His will. At best, you may find the whole of life but a winter; but you will soon pass the solstice; spiritually speaking, the nights will be getting less, and the days a little longer; soon, soon we shall hear the celestial harmonies which usher in the everlasting spring. Be enamored of a spiritual life, and let God take His own method of producing it. Be not weary of your trials; look upon them all as certainly of His ordering, and find your relief daily in pouring out your heart to Him concerning them. Pray, my dear child, pray simply. Life, peace, victory over sin, success in every good work depend on prayer. Never doubt that there may be such a union with Christ as shall cause life to flow from Him to you as naturally as water from a fountain. He will always give us according to our wants when those wants are spread before Him in faith. The first, and indeed we may say the only condition to our receiving the blessing, is to be able fully to cast our burden, whatever it may be, upon the Lord with faith that He hears us and will help us.

VI.

In our progress through Time, what an unceasing effort there is in our souls to rise *above* it, and to breathe the atmosphere of Heaven. In this effort we have been united for several years, and every difficulty surmounted, every new victory over our foes and fears is made doubly joyous from knowing that it is in one sense a mutual victory. Thus I have felt for a few weeks past that you were with me on the mount, while, like Moses on Pisgah, I have seemed to see the promised land. I have been made to understand also that no way could have conducted me to it but the very way of "the wilderness," into which, in times past, I have so often feared I had been led not in mercy, but in judgment.

I must tell you that there is a way, as yet but partially revealed to you, by which you will find all that life, and freedom, and peace, and fruitfulness, you have ever hoped for. Be not dismayed by any present perplexities. The things which seem to be against you have all been so arranged by Divine wisdom as to work in the end most effectually for you. O, could I only impress upon you the single thought, that to trust God's love when you are most sensibly unworthy of it, is to Him a more grateful sacrifice, an offering of a sweeter savor, than to give your body to be burned under the shadow of a notion that you thereby render yourself particularly acceptable to Him. Never, never, have I had such a sense of the absolute freedom with which the *choicest* blessings are given. Do you not see at a glance that the thorough belief of this is the one thing essential to the life of prayer? Once get hold of this, and then pray on—pray ever. * * * * You have indeed been crossed in your strongest natural desires, and you are enclosed in a situation which yields but little pleasure, and presents much difficulty; and thus has God always dealt with His chosen. When He delivered the children of Israel from their bondage in Egypt He might have given them the possession of that country, and the full enjoyment of all its dignities and treasures, and with this they would have been better pleased than with the course He actually adopted.

When He delivered you from the slavery of guilt He might at the same time have opened a path to worldly ease and affluence, and enjoyment; but instead of that, He has led you in a way of weariness, toil, trial, and mortification, and why? Because He designed something far better for you than you then could even comprehend, or than you yet perhaps dare confidently to appropriate. * * * * * The folly of the Israelites consisted in not being wholly reconciled to the Divine plan, in only half believing God's gracious assurances, and hence murmuring under the disappointments of their earthly desires. All we want is faith to follow wholly in the new and strange path which grace has opened before us, however trying to nature, to be so reconciled to our trials that they shall cease to be trials. By meditating constantly on the nature and promises of God, we shall get after a while such a sense of their excellence, and such an assurance of our interest in them, that we shall not desire a single addition to our worldly blessings.

Let it be enough that God has shown us the vanity of earthly things, yea, their misery, as it is difficult to possess them without being in bondage to them. He has given us an infinitely better portion; He has made us His children; He has assured us of heaven, and of His grace to conduct us thither; and besides this, He will never leave us to want any worldly good, which will not hinder our progress heavenward, or which we are prepared to use for His glory.

There is no consolation with reference to our worldly affairs, unless we can say with simplicity, "The Lord will provide;" and I trust that we can say this with faith. Yet how strange it is that we can trust God so easily with the greater concerns of our souls, and be so doubtful of the less. Endeavor in the most simple manner to cast all your care on the Lord. How easy for Him to help you; how like Him to disappoint your fears. Be sure that God has nothing for you in the future but blessing, if you will dismiss every care but that of trusting Him. Your minutest wants are His care. If you may only grow in the spirit of submission, trust, and prayer, throw every other care to the winds, or rather quietly leave all with Him. * * * * * You probably feel nothing but your unworthiness, and therefore fear; but expect much from God on the score of *His* faithfulness to simple, trusting, self-renouncing faith. Christian faithfulness is the free response of our hearts to the invitations and promises of God's grace. You can do all things in such a faith. I have small concern for you, not because I do not love you, or sympathize with you, but because I know so well Him who loves you infinitely. and I think I see something of His particular designs for you. Indeed after the experience which I have reached on the subject of Providence, I have a secret joy, as in my own trials, so in those of my dearest friends.

I predict that your heavenly possessions will henceforth be felt to be nearer and more real than they were ever felt to be before. There is a kind of certainty in regard to the love of God which we may attain without affliction, but I refer to something very different from this. We may know (in a sense) that we are the owners of a treasure which is worth more than all the world beside, but it is locked up in a casket where we never or scarcely ever get a clear sight of it, or it may be held for us until we come to a certain age, or it may lie far off in a foreign land, and all the comfort we have in it may come from the belief that sometime or other we shall enter upon its actual possession and full enjoyment. Affliction sweeps away all these interposing conditions. The truth is, they exist only in our unbelief. Our hearts are so satisfied with the present, with our earthly possessions, that we have not felt the necessity of considering deeply either the certainty or the value of the heavenly.

I have been thinking within a few days of the passage "God so *loved* the world that He gave His only begotten Son," and it seems almost as though I never had any heart conception of that love before.

And now, my dear friend, remembering that "the highest earthly happiness is still a flower that blossoms upon thorns," let us seek for enduring joy only in God. In bonds of tenderest, indissoluble sympathy, your friend—

VII.

YOU will think, I am afraid, that though I write to you at "sundry times" it is certainly not in "divers manners;" but I am constantly on a strain to teach you a certain truth which, after all, you can only learn by experience—a certain grace, rather—patience in trial. I once had the idea which I suppose every novice in Christianity has, that the great mountain which stands in the way of spiritual progress—self-will—was to be removed by one sufficiently bold and decisive exercise of faith; that in some favored moment a stream of Divine illumination, bursting on my long-strained and waiting vision, would dislodge the enemy forever, and make all further conflict unnecessary. Shall I say I hold to this still? If I do, it is certainly with very important qualifications.

It was after the disciples had rowed hard the whole night, barely escaping shipwreck by so doing, that Jesus appeared at the fourth watch. They would not have been saved if they had stopped rowing, and all their rowing would not have saved them if Jesus had not at last appeared. Your daily exercises and efforts may seem very unmeaning; they seem to bring you no nearer to the great deliverance. You are tempted constantly to give up in despair; you cannot conceive how such miserable prayers can avail anything; but just continue in them, still animated, however faintly, by the hopes of the appearance of Jesus. What can I say more to make you certain of His coming at your fourth watch?

* * * Trial means anything which discovers our weakness—our helpless impotency to rise—our apparently hopeless barrenness. I have never had any other trial which I could not easily bear in comparison with this. But this life-long burden of selfishness! How we suffer "from its jeal-

ousies and anxieties, its exaggerations of the good and extenuations of the evil within us, its shrinkings from the cross, its impatience under the consciousness of defects, its yearnings for perfection without the slow process of mortification, its slowness to surrender everything to the will of God." How partial it makes us in our beliefs. In our early Christian life especially, how apt we are, under the blinding power of selfishness, to take a part of the word of God for the whole—the part which favors us. It opens our eyes wide, perhaps, to the grace of God, but blinds us to His holiness. It makes us think (in spite of our better judgment) that we may be happy without being holy, *entirely* holy, at least. We make reserves for some secret, selfish affection, and if we are the children of God, we shall always be in trouble while this is the case. Oh, the blessedness of that state in which selfishness is no longer known!

My best direction to you in bearing these trials is the one I have so often given you before—keep continually applying the doctrine of a free justification. Learn to dissociate them from all question as to your state in the sight of God. Do not look upon your continued weakness and the trials it occasions as a proof simply of your obstinate sinfulness, but as God's gracious method of healing you. *Bear* them, simply bear them, relying on His wisdom and love to give you the victory in His own time and way. Be sure that it is not the attainment, but the struggle for it, by constant faith, and hope, and patience, and prayer, which makes you well pleasing to God.

Relief will come at last, as to some extent it has come already, not by any direct consciousness of sanctification, so much as by an increasing consciousness of the love of God in your free and absolute justification which will make you sure of whatever you ask for in the way of an ever-growing nearness and likeness to Him. Then you will not only be reconciled to trials—you will rejoice in them. You will want nothing so much as that God will discover more and more of your weakness, and keep on purging you till you are wholly pure. You will ask for nothing but patience to submit more perfectly to His will, till at length the very sense of suffering shall be absorbed in a joyful allegiance to Him in all circumstances.

How I wish you could have heard the sermon which I heard yesterday from the Rev. Mr. M——

an Englishman, on the sacrifice of Isaac, or rather the faith and obedience of Abraham—the angelic clearness with which the preacher illustrated all those truths which I, like a clumsy mechanic, have been trying to teach you—the distinction between life as a free gift, and the *crown* of life as the reward of endurance, an endurance only possible to those who receive life as a gift. How you would have been confirmed forever in all that you have heard from your humble teacher. And when he talked of temptation, its nature and design, how it would have scattered all your concern on the subject of sanctification, by showing you that your present trials, arising from a consciousness of weakness, endured by faith in Christ alone, were the very means by which God was leading you to the crown.

For my own part, if I lived ten miles from Philadelphia, I should think it nothing to walk in every Saturday to hear one of that man's sermons, which are mainly expositions of Scripture. He is a real genius, and full of natural eloquence, equally remarkable for the solidity of his thoughts, and for the logical clearness with which he delivers them, without a scrap of paper. But what most amazes me about him is his knowledge of Scripture. He talks like a man who alone among men had received the Divine revelation—like a man to whom every other book, even as a means of interpreting this, was nonsense. I have heard two other sermons or expositions from him equally remarkable, but I have not time for details.

Hold fast your faith then, dear child. I learn daily that *concern* about sanctification is not the way to advance in it. Let it drop out of your cares, and be filled only with thoughts of Christ's love to you—His mysterious love. In a little while you will be filled with it, and that will be your sanctification.

VIII.

GOD in His wise and holy Providence, which I have no doubt is most merciful, too, has brought me very near to death ; and to you as one of the earliest, and one of the truest friends I have had on earth, to whom I have been bound as I have been to few by a religious sympathy, and as to one especially who may receive some benefit from such a communication, I will tell what transpired between my soul and God, after like Hezekiah, I had "turned my face to the wall," with nothing before me but eternity. I have a doctrine to proclaim to you which you know, which we have both known, which more than any other lies at the foundation of Christian experience, but which has been brought home to me recently with a power of which I never had any experience before. It is only for setting this doctrine in the clearest light that I must give you an outline of my spiritual history for some time past. For some months, before I had any apprehension of serious disease, I have had a clearer conviction of sin—of the power of sin—as an element of all my past history, and of its ill-desert, than I have ever had before. My former convictions have sometimes been attended with as strong emotions, but never have the nature, root, causes, and aggravations of sin made such a deep impression upon my understanding. Never has the very *core* of sin (self-regard instead of regard to Christ, and to man for Christ's sake, and in imitation of His example) and its ramifications through all my conduct, been an object of such distinct, fearfully distinct vision. My convictions have never before blotted out or made so completely useless all *evidences* of regeneration.

Though I have aimed and resolved not to live to myself, yet in all my particular means, instruments, and methods of action, I have been so much perverted and deceived by this principle of self-regard, I have offended in short so habitually in particular actions, that I cannot but consider myself as having broken the whole law—not of Sinai, but of Calvary; the want of *love* runs through the whole tissue.

About my bodily malady I have had little concern; another concern, infinitely more terrible, took possession of me in the hours of my deep retirement. Conscience was stirred to its lowest depths. As by a flash of lightning from the judgment seat, I was prostrated by a clear apprehension of sin. My whole heart was laid open, and it seemed to be nothing but a nest of vipers; my whole life seemed nothing but one tissue of corruption. I saw all the good there was about it as clearly as ever; my perpetual struggle with evil, the many manifestations I have had of God's favor, my successes over particular temptations; but I saw that all these were very superficial and comparatively external, as evidences of a justified or sanctified state. All past experiences I utterly renounced. I did not want to be saved in virtue of such miserable stuff. I wanted a real salvation, —a salvation direct from God, in perfect harmony with His perfections, given not merely because I was a miserable, perishing creature, the proper object of compassion (though I made much of that plea), but because He could give it justly and holily.

The only particle of light that gave me any hope here was Christ's sacrificial suffering. I must now *prove* the virtue, the full virtue, of the one great Sacrifice. Nothing else could give me confidence in death, which seemed so near. O, my thirst, my thirst for the living water—for the powerful influence of the Spirit—for one ray from the loving countenance of God, enabling me to perceive the all-sufficiency of the sacrifice for sin, as I saw my desert of its penalty. Forgiveness, forgiveness, that is what I want! Shall I obtain it, coming as a sinner, *with nothing but sin*, the sin of a whole life, peculiarly aggravated, and most vividly apprehended? Is Christ alone a sufficient foundation for the hope of a sinner in the hour of death, in the moment of judgment; and shall that be verified to me by the breathing of the Spirit of love upon my heart; by a Divine response to the cry of my perishing spirit? These were the questions.

What I wanted was forgiveness, but not that alone—not merely a sure deliverance from wrath, but some sign of the love of the Father and the grace of the Saviour, whose frown was eternal sorrow, grief without remedy. God appeared to me not at all as an angry despot, but as a most loving Father, and Christ as my loving Saviour. The dread which was upon my spirit was not of some mysterious penalty in another world, an infliction of evil, but of separation from the source of all love—from the bosom of a Father, and particularly from that blessed Being who had given His life for man.

How clear it now became to me that Christ came into the world, that He came especially, eminently, above every other part of His mission, for the purpose of dying for sin—for the purpose of taking the sinner's place in the eye of law and justice, so that the sinner could feel that there was no moral necessity for his punishment, and that God could be just and yet forgive him boundlessly. I could no longer doubt that this is just what all those scriptural expressions about Christ's dying for us, mean. I could not avoid seeing that if that is not the Gospel, it would be no more suited to one in my condition, which is at some time or other the universal condition, than a code of morals. I knew that God was good, loving, merciful; but I just as well knew, and at present far more impressively, that He was just also. Of the possibility of forgiveness in a way of righteousness, then, I had not the slightest misgiving. It was all my comfort.

Thus planting myself anew on the Rock of Ages, all my concern was lulled. I could not resist the conviction that God looked upon me as a child, an *invalid* child. That, though I had not been successful in my struggle against sin, He accepted the *struggle* as the true test of my character, and that all my personal sufferings were but his Fatherly chastisements intended for my purification—not for retribution. And how overwhelmingly was this view corroborated by the Scriptures, which now poured into me like a flood! How could I have expected anything else from that Being who, though the Holy One, is represented as so pitiful, so tender, so long-suffering toward *sinners*, and particularly when, by every such display of kindness, He honors His Son, who was our sin-bearer, as much as He blesses us—and constrains us to honor Him also.

I know not what is before me. My head, though relieved, is not whole; but the sting of sin has gone. Thanks be to God who giveth me the victory. My peace is without interruption. "Whom He loveth He chasteneth," satisfies every doubt, and gives a kind of pleasure to the pain. I love to endure what His loving hand lays upon me. My sky seems cloudless as I advance. The everlasting love illumines alike both worlds. In my Father's house are many mansions. * * * * One part of my discipline much harder than my diet of herbs, has been to be obliged to intermit my correspondence with you. May the Good Shepherd lead you in green pastures and by still waters.

IX.

I AM deeply affected by your generosity in writing so long and so kind a letter to me while walking yourself in the shadow of God's holy Providences. It greatly cheers me to find you so calm and submissive under such a trial. I have thought that silence might express my sympathy better than words. Since you have permitted me, however, I am glad to speak, and particularly of the more inward trouble under which you labor, which seems easily explained, upon principles which of late have taken a strong hold upon my mind, and perhaps may have been permitted to do so for the purpose in part of helping you in your perplexity. * * * * * I find the radical evil of my nature to be the *undue love of self*, an inordinate regard to my own happiness. This is my original sin, the cause of all wrong feeling and wrong doing in respect both to God and man. A single glance at the moral law might teach us this truth, but it is only the discipline of Providence that makes us feel it. Men in general never blame themselves for making their own happiness their end, but only for the ways in which they seek it; and even the Christian, until he becomes very spiritual, thinks there can be no error in seeking his own happiness, or in making it his end, provided he seeks it in communion with God, or in the enjoyment of the Divine favor. But I apprehend that the original law of our nature goes below this, and requires us to cease from all thought about our own happiness, the end which deserves all our thoughts being out of ourselves, in aiming at which simply, we are happy necessarily without our own care.

Even if I can say with truth that I find all my happiness in the sense of God's favor, yet if that is my *end*, even in part, instead of the doing and suffering God's holy will, which alone is worthy of all my regard, then I am but imperfectly conformed to the law of my nature. I am, so far, unholy; I do not love God with all my heart, nor render Him the glory which is His due.

It is true that we are so made that we cannot but desire our own happiness; but God, who gave us this constitution, gave us also all the happiness of which we were capable, by making us *His children.* Think what that means. As children of such a Father, what a wrong we should do to Him in cherishing any concern about our own happiness; and particularly in turning aside from His commands, whatever they might be, to take care of ourselves. This is the whole of sin. The penalty immediately follows in the soul's sensible exclusion from the privileges of a child, without any abatement of its obligations as a subject of

Law. Providing for itself, which once gave it no care, becomes now unavoidably its whole care, and it must obey all the commandments of God beside. In this condition the Law only aggravates the evil, turns the soul into a sink of selfishness, and makes God, if thought of at all, an object of hatred. This is the condition in which the Gospel finds us. *Though sinners*, it reinvests us at once with all the privileges of children. Christ undertaking to provide for our happiness, we have nothing to do but to love. Believing in the office and promise of Christ to this effect, we are at once free. As to privilege, we are just where we were before we sinned; God is our Father, so completely reconciled, that we have no more reason to question His love to us, or to expect anything but good from Him, than the angels have. This is our justification.

But in ourselves, we are not just what we were before we sinned. Unbelief, and its correlate selfishness, are in us not merely as a tendency, but as a principle—a habit, a character, which in our present state can only be changed by degrees. Thus to change us, gradually to bring us back to perfect love to Him, is the end of all His dealings with us which often " are for the present not joyous but grievous."

Now we know that God's end in all His dealings with His people must be to make them holy. His love obliges Him to this, for it is the only way of making them really happy; and if holiness includes the perfect subordination of all our desires, even our desires for spiritual enjoyment, to the desire of doing and suffering His holy will, is it not plain what his object is in withholding the sense of His favor in certain cases—in those cases, viz., where there is danger that His communications may be more valued than Himself?

Do you remember the words of Madame Guyon, whose religious experience is one of the deepest and richest that we have upon record? "I did not then understand," is her language, "that in the progress of the inward death, I must be crucified not only to the joys of sense, and the pleasures of worldly vanity, but also, which is a more terrible and trying crucifixion, that I must *die to the joys of God*, in order that I might live to the will of God."

Such, indeed, is God's compassion as well as wisdom, that He will not try His people in this way beyond what they are able to bear. His end both in giving to the weak, and in withholding from the strong is to advance their holiness. Some years ago such a trial as you are now enduring would probably have destroyed you—now it will be the means of your rapid improvement. In a word, our holiness, as a general rule, is the measure of our capacity for communion with God, and of course for spiritual joy; and to make us receptive of the highest and the most glorious communications, God often withholds the sense of His favor from those whom He has prepared to bear such a discipline, that in the absence of all joy inward and outward, they may cleave to *Him* by faith alone, and thus make those advances in holiness, or in the capacity for spiritual enjoyment, which can be made in no other way.

Nothing can be plainer to me, therefore, than that in submitting to this inward as well as to the outward rod, as intended for the wisest and kindest purposes, and as certain to be in its result only a rich blessing, against every kind of evidence to the contrary, you are exercising Abram's faith, and shall certainly have his reward, "you shall have a *new name*."

You have nothing to do but to thirst, just as you are now thirsting, only with increasing desire for a manifestation of Christ to your soul, together with perfect submission while it is withheld ; that is, when you have really died, not only to all other joy but union with Him, but have died also even to your desire for His special manifestation, then, O what joy awaits you! You must so believe that He is all goodness itself, as to be able to say from your very heart, "His mere promise is just as good as a personal conscious experience," all the while, however, desiring that experience as you desire nothing else, *except His glory*—that you must desire above all personal good.

Confide in Him, my dear friend, not only that He will give you the victory in a little while, but that He will support you, that He is now supporting you, and will through the conflict. He cannot fail. From the Word of God, and your own ineradicable want, the idea has been begotten in the depths of your being of a Bridegroom of the soul. That idea is the key which opens heaven—will open it to you at length.

X.

THOUGH my circumstances are not very favorable at present for correspondence, I cannot rest until I have replied at least briefly to your letter. It concerns me to hear you talk as you do about the Atonement, as though you knew nothing about it—had everything to learn, etc. Doubtless you were speaking of the philosophy of the Atonement.

I wish you could act upon the impression (as I wish I always could myself), which I have no doubt we both have strongly enough, the really little importance of a philosophy of religion, to say nothing of the danger of an eager desire for it. Let us be grateful for the teachings of the Spirit, that is for our experience. Have we not, under a sense of the ill desert of sin, and in our despair of help from any reason-taught method, joyfully rested in the *testimony of God* concerning the way of deliverance by the Propitiatory Sacrifice? All the light which we may ever get from study (though useful) will do but little to establish our understandings in comparison with this which comes through a spiritual experience; and even in presenting the truth successfully to others, the confidence inspired by this spiritual experience will do vastly more than any clearness of statement.

I can assure you that all your difficulties of this nature arise from expecting reason to do the work of faith. The mysteries of the Gospel are hidden from the wise and are revealed unto babes. The natural man, that is, the merely intellectual man, receiveth not the things of God—the doctrines of the Gospel—because they are discerned by another principle, spiritually; I mean the principle of faith. From the first announcement of the purpose of redemption down to the present hour, the work has been carried on by this principle alone; and in every age, and in every heart, this work has been slow or rapid, dubious or clear, according to the degree in which this principle has prevailed. Faith is at once the reproach and the glory of the Christian system; its reproach, because to one condition of the human mind it is foolishness; its glory, because to another condition, it is the power of God. Faith is simply a reliance on the Word of God, in preference to the dictates of our natural wisdom, and in opposition to the current of our earthly passions.

The more we employ our reason simply, upon the ideas of sin, Divine justice, grace, etc., as presented in the Gospel, the more we shall get confused. But by becoming children, that is, by exercising submission and confidence (upon proper and sufficient grounds, of course), we receive the light gradually which makes the Divine dispensations clearer. The chief difficulty with you has been, if I mistake not, that you want to see immediately and perfectly what is the result of a great deal of discipline, reflection, and experience. I doubt whether you will ever *see* clearly (in this world, at least), the justice and benevolence of God in the permission of sin, or in causing the whole race to suffer for the offense of one individual. But you can *believe* that the Judge of all the earth does right—that God is holy in all His ways, and righteous in all His works. You *can* leave these questions as not belonging to you, and employ your mind upon the nature of sin (considered in itself and without respect to its origin), and upon the merciful provision which God has made for our redemption.

In this way you will gradually acquire such powerful impressions of the Divine holiness, justice, and benignity, that though those other points may still remain mysterious, they will not affect your estimate of the Divine character, nor damp in the slightest degree, your feelings of love and devotion. Let the matter of all your concern be, that you found your whole hope upon the truth that we are saved not at all by our own wisdom, or our own righteousness, but entirely through faith in Christ the Mediator. Your trials will all arise from the speculative spirit, and from the legal spirit—in other words from your own wisdom and your own righteousness. They must be brought down and cast out, and in proportion as they are you will know experimentally what is meant by the "mystery" which Paul preached: "Christ in you the hope of glory."

I am coming to rest rapidly, my brother, since I have learned how little the understanding has to do in attaining the true knowledge of God—in other words, how much unrest there is and must needs be in scientific theology. The only pure theology is the mystical, which each soul must attain for itself through Divine discipline. Scientific or church theology may be indeed an outer court, but there is no rest or perfect union with God till we get *through* it; then we reach the Holy of Holies which has no want left but to be absent from the body.

I sympathize with you most deeply in what you say of the "danger of life-barrenness." We have great reason to be humbled for our want of those traits of Christian character which tend directly to the outward diffusion of Christianity. Yet it is the absence of those deeper traits of Christian character which give to the outward life all its value in God's sight, that we should specially lament. I must believe that the essence of Christianity lies in gracious *affections*. To grow in these should be our chief desire—our ruling passion, so to speak—a passion which should be nurtured by reading and reflection, and, above all, by prayer. I know no other means. How, but by the spirit of grace, which is given to importunate prayer (and therefore not immediately), can we know sin and love in their fearful contrast?

We talk, or many do, of serving Christ, and far be it from me to discourage such, for I have no doubt that Christ accepts and will greatly reward the smallest service; but if I should express my want in a word, it is that I might *sympathize* with

Christ—that I might have the most thorough fellowship with His sufferings—that I might see sin and love as they can be seen only in His humiliation and suffering for our sake—that I might be ever reading my condemnation and my deliverance in those crimson lines: thus to be crucified with Christ, and yet to live, is my idea of Christian perfection. Does not holiness consist in entire deadness to self, the heart having been made alive unto God? which is just when we see that in the sacrifice of His Son, He has rendered superfluous all our sacrifices. But shall we give Him nothing in return? Can we help giving our whole selves to Him?

I can give you no idea, my dear brother, of the plentitude of my confidence for you, notwithstanding you are often a prey to doubt, and your conceptions of faith and its privileges are, in some respects, I must believe, yet imperfect.

I am busily engaged in writing a sermon on unbelief. O that by this I might strike a blow which would liberate many a soul from the power of darkness! Its commencement and its progress, indeed, was attended with much heart-searching trial. Of late I have been able, by reason of beginning with much higher assurance than formerly, to go far more deeply into myself. Is there any greater rapture on earth than the Christian experiences when, even in the midst of the most vivid realization of his own unworthiness and unfaithfulness, he finds that it has not estranged the heart of God from him?

XI.

I HAVE preached all day in the hardest church for a speaker in the city, and yet I feel impelled to undertake a third service in replying to your most delightful letter, trusting that love may supply the defect of bodily vigor. "Behold how He loved him," said the spectators of the scene at Bethany. There are no spectators of my heart's movements, or they might say the same. No day passes, my dear brother, without a sweet and often a solemn remembrance of our past intercourse, nor without a feeling of joy in the prospect of seeing you again.

But there was something in your last letter which has greatly deepened my interest in you. Our *communion in Christ*, which I have always felt to be a very close one, is more perfect, I am persuaded, than I had hitherto supposed. Theoretic differences, which I imagine divided us a little, appear to be thoroughly melted by the spiritual convictions which we possess in common, and which are ever becoming deeper in both of us. Our experiences are modified but very little by difference of circumstances, and not at all, I apprehend, by difference of culture. Both in our consciousness of sin as a leprosy, and of daily help from the promise and power of Christ, producing a determination to "know nothing else," and perpetual prayer that our union with Him may be complete and perfect, that thus we may live wholly unto God—in these, the main features of our experience, we are entirely one.

But the most interesting thing in your letter is the manner in which you speak of your confidence in salvation. No; the most interesting thing is of a painful kind: it relates to your trials in preaching. I know all about it from the most thorough experience—often bitter experience. I was deeply touched by that passage in your letter, in which you ask my prayers that God will give you strength to conquer and rule your nature. It will encourage you to know that this has for some time been precisely the language of my prayers for you. Your nature, I well know, is most excitable, and it labors to realize a very high ideal in all things. This makes it certain that your life is to be one of stern conflict. So deeply do I sympathize with you, both in your present condition, and in your prospect, that it seems to me I might be willing, accustomed as I have been to endurance, to assume and appropriate a portion of your trials, if thereby they might be made lighter to yourself. But all I can do is to give you encouragement, and that I do on the firmest conviction that God is speaking through me—that I am not uttering my own hopes merely, but am in a degree inspired as Ananias was to assure Paul that while he should suffer great things for the Gospel's sake, he should be sustained by all the Divine love and faithfulness.

Your "two points" have been my two points all my life. From the beginning, the consciousness of my low spiritual attainments has been my great burden. Nothing else has given me such perplexity, and caused such discouragement in my efforts to do good to others. How I have writhed and struggled, and spent *all* my struggles (wasting a great deal) in the effort to get on higher ground myself. I see now very plainly that Satan has been in much of my earnestness on this subject, or rather in my restiveness—for the subject demands an earnestness, but ambition and pride made it restiveness. I am sure you are far better guarded against his wiles than I was at the same period of my ministry. I hope you have also a much stronger support than I had generally, in another kind of consciousness, viz.: of the integrity of your heart, and of the Divine presence and favor. My consolation in regard to all my failures (public) is that they were all a private gain. Through such losses I think my soul has been saved. Obliged by the fury of the storm to throw everything overboard, my little bark seems at length to be going straight toward the heavenly port. Yours will go in, I trust, with more of a cargo.

It gives me the greatest delight to notice the trust and submission which breathe in the general tone of your letter. Oh, my dear brother, allow nothing to come between you and Christ. I assure you, cares about your own qualifications and work are more likely to mislead you than anything else. You have certainly a great trial to go through, arising from a keen sense which you have of your own poverty; but this very trial will be the making of you, if you bow your neck to it, and find your comfort in the faithfulness of Christ.

Therefore, O man, greatly beloved, fear not! Peace be unto thee! Be strong; yea, be strong (Dan. x. 19). The very thing on which your heart is set, a higher order of inward life, a more thorough absorption of Christ's spirit and Christ's truth, is the thing which your Lord is preparing for you; and exceeding abundantly above what you are asking for will be bestowed. Work on, in the confidence that your present afflictions are working for you a boundless bliss. Can there be any doubt of it? God will not suffer you to fail.

I want very much to talk with you more at length than I have time for now, on your "second point"—the subject of your prayer—that you may be led into more active service for Christ. It is true that we cannot move till the pillar of glory rises from its resting-place and goes before us. But I apprehend that we must *watch* with diligence while we pray. As there is danger on the one hand of assuming more than we have strength to perform, so there is on the other of shrinking from responsibility.

After all, the great work is to grow in faith and love. Exercise will indeed help our growth, but aliment is the main thing. Aliment without exercise will make us indolent; but exercise without sufficient aliment will soon wear us down. The idea of service (regarded as a means of increasing strength) may easily occupy too much of our minds. The disinterested or direct desire of serving Christ cannot be too strong; but to promote it, the main thing is to become more deeply acquainted with Christ—to see more of his glory. This is what I mean by aliment.

I wish I had time to tell you about the meetings of thrilling interest which I have attended since I came to New York—to one of which I must hasten now. The revival is increasing rather than diminishing. I meet constantly a great number of friends—friends of years, who give evidence of deep and unusual feeling on religious subjects, and others of a want of feeling, and I must not leave till I have used what influence I have to encourage the one and awaken the other.

I attended the 12 o'clock prayer-meeting in Fulton street, yesterday, and never was in such a scene before—such singing, such exhortations, such prayers, I never heard. People who generally had no previous knowledge of each other, all of them of most respectable appearance—by far the majority assumed in all the exercises to be impenitent, some of them earnestly entreating prayers for themselves, some for dear relatives: and among them, what was my emotion in discerning a young, aspiring lawyer, the youngest son of one of the dearest friends of my former years, for whom, on his father's account as well as his own, I had long yearned, especially since he came from the West to this vortex of sin. For his sake alone I would stay here a fortnight, if necessary. But there are other cases equally interesting, and the one on whose account I came far more so.

Let us go on our way, my brother, in the firm confidence, that in closely following the Divine guidance, walking by faith every day, we shall be saved. We shall not fall in the wilderness, but go forward, and get through. There is more meaning in that word, *trusting*, than we commonly think.

It is in one sense the hardest thing a creature can do, but *the* thing, and the only thing, which makes our salvation sure. And yet we must not trust in our trust specially. Here lies a great danger and difficulty. When we are cast out (in our own apprehension), naked, and helpless, and desperate, and still trust Christ, though we probably shall not have the slightest reflection on our exercise of trusting, we then have the promise " to them that have no might He increaseth strength."

XII.

THE night is long, but the morning cometh. This has been the text of all my letters. I cannot alter God's ways toward you, but with His blessing, I may be able to make you understand them better, so that long and dark as the night may be, you may still be animated by the hope of awaking in Heaven.

And what is Heaven? When the love illusions of time shall be transformed into unchanging, eternal, and ever-shining manifestations of God's love to the soul. Is there any conception of Heaven more true to nature and to the Scriptures than this? Let me show you then, on Scriptural principles, which are therefore undeniable, the connection between such a state and your present trials. How did these trials begin, and what is their nature? Have they not their root in the unalterable normal law of your nature, that you can find your life only in love? and in the division of your heart, at present between two objects of desire, without a clear and full ability of enjoying either? The world, you believe, will prove an illusion, while the love of God you know, objectively at least, to be a perfect reality; but your enjoyment of the latter is so partial, and unsatisfying, that you cannot entirely shake off your dependence upon the other. How the obstacle which you call "loving the world" has been overcome in my case, you want to know, rightly judging that I must have had an experience in this matter very similar to your own.

Truly, truly, for many long years the essence and root of all my troubles lay in what seemed to be an entirely uncontrollable love of the world. For long, long years, I felt that nothing could divorce me from this love, but some violent catastrophe. The more I was commanded by conscience not to covet, the more absolutely I loved. How was I delivered? The story is a very simple one. When that sweet voice came to me, "Neither do I condemn thee," the charm was dissolved. For many years that sweet voice has been sounding in my heart, still so strange, that if I should listen to any other interpretation of it but that of my own nature and experience, it would pass for nothing; but its effect, as well as its scriptural basis, proves it Divine. The Gospel which saves me, which delivers me from all my troubles is simply this: "My child. I know your nature, for I am the Author of it, and that nature in all its demands shall be fully satisfied. But you mistake in supposing that the world could give you the satisfaction you desire, even if you possessed all it could give. But I will do it. I now give you my absolute promise, that what you have been so long pining for (and which, though you have mistaken its formal object, is the demand of a true nature), you shall yet possess beyond the dreams of fiction. I could, at once, make such a revelation of myself to you as would deliver you from all further uncertainty. But this would tend rather to your own exaltation than mine—and, therefore, for this, as well as for other reasons, I must do it by a process of discipline. Guided and supported by faith in my love, and in the promise of my coming at the proper season, I must leave you to struggle for a while with the evils of your nature, and, however obstinate those evils may prove, let this be your unfailing refuge, that I am with you, *never* hereafter to *condemn*, but only to pity and pardon, and with every temptation to make a way of escape." Read John xvii. from verse 18 to the end, and wonder.

I do not mean that from total bondage I was suddenly ushered into daylight and freedom, nor that the Gospel, as above stated, which has given me a perfect rest from my misery, came to me at once by a sudden manifestation. I always had a little of it mixed with a much larger proportion of legalism, which neutralized its virtue, but which by the trials of years has been purged away, leaving between myself and Christ the simple relation of unchanging love, and unquestioning confidence.

You feel that the great obstacle to your sanctification lies in the strength of certain natural desires, and you are forever making, or thinking you ought to make, assaults upon your *nature*, to make it fit for the indwelling of Christ, as though there was a change to precede as well as to follow such indwelling. Now I conceive the great peculiarity of Christ to be, that He is exactly suited to our nature as it is, embracing all its wants. Our most immediate want is deliverance from penalty, and from the fear of it, which we have been taught is obtained gratuitously, by faith in the provisions of the atonement. But this (by itself) is only the lifting off of an external pressure. Deeper and stronger than the sense of wrath is the infirmity and corruption of the soul itself, the incessant gravitation of the affections toward a false center, known to be false. We want sanctification. Are you not conscious that your deepest want is not of affection merely, but of affection combined with purity—the love of a nature which in loving will purify and exalt you? It is not peace, simply, that you seek, but peace unto purification.

By a necessity which no power of will can change, your affections (I speak of the natural state), are made, as you cannot but know, to find their alliance with the All-True, the All-Good, the All-Fair. Here is the whole of your trouble ; your heart is perishing for love, but made distrustful by sin of the only Being whose love can satisfy you, it is ever tempted to seek a substitute for His affection in visions of earthly bliss, which however warmly you may pursue, you know you can never find in such sufficiency, and in such purity, as your nature requires, in the world. "O, were there but a love which could perfectly satisfy the heart, without forever disturbing the repose of the conscience!" This is your cry. Do you not know that the radical idea of Christianity is to meet this want, and do you not feel that if Christianity is worth anything to you it must meet it?

What, then, is the difficulty? Plainly, your supposing a condition to this attainment which your experience makes it perfectly certain you can never perform,—some *change of nature;* whereas, the very thing which changes your nature, (that is, gives you a power over its lower affinities,) is its coming by faith into direct union with the object which satisfies its highest demands. Christ received not merely as a general Benefactor, but as a Personal Friend, just as the Scriptures tender Him, and as your personal experience testifies that you need Him—Christ received into your heart, *is* your sanctification.

He descends to you in your unhappy state, and gives you the assurance that He loves you with a love which can never change. He tells you that He has begun to deliver you from the bondage of corruption ; that you are encircled by the arms of His love and wisdom, of which the one shall direct, and the other support you, through all the trials of your pilgrimage path. You have seen God in the *face* of *Jesus Christ*. You have beheld Him. Love itself, a living, personal being, able and willing to meet and satisfy all your longings, both for love and for purity. He has proved His love for you by dying for you. "For a good man some would even dare to die," but to love those who are utterly unworthy of it, whom *dying* for them could hardly win, and to persevere in loving them, notwithstanding his clear and constant perception of their unworthiness, O, how different from the love of man!—and this is the distinguishing characteristic of your Heavenly, Eternal Friend.

You have had an idea that the fellowship which Christ offers you is burdened with difficult conditions. But depend upon it, this is an entire misconception. The primary requirement of the Gospel is, that you should repose with unchanging confidence on Christ's love to you—the only love or service desired or expected of you, being such as this faith will secure, according to its strength, spontaneously generated. The real demand is for faith in His love, under all possible conditions.

Do you not believe that if this view, which contains the quintessence of the Gospel, instead of being a theory merely, were to become a vital reality (which it will become exactly in proportion as you act upon it), you would be able to reply, with Peter, to the question of the Saviour, "Lovest thou me?" "Lord, Thou knowest that I love Thee?" Answer directly from your consciousness, as Peter did, in view simply of the report which the Gospel brings of the person of Christ, and His love to you. Do you suppose that Peter's answer, which you cannot doubt was a true one, and most acceptable to the Master, was founded upon the *proofs* which he had given of his love (a singular test for him); or that it was the result of a particular self-examination, and of the discovery of some tolerable conformity between his life and his obligation? Is it not obvious upon the slightest reflection that it was simply a burst of feeling, quickened by a sense of his miserable failures, and the amazingly manifested love of such a superior Being to one wholly unworthy?

And now, my dear friend, let me exhort you to hang your whole salvation, your whole soul, with all its interests and its needs, upon the word and love of Him who gave His life for you, and who has gone into Heaven to prepare a place for you there. Though conscience may still storm, and the devil in angelic garb try to beguile, such a faith as that must be effectual against the world, and Satan, and self, not by its own power, which is nothing, but by its power to move your loving Lord.

Be sure to ask me any questions which may arise in your mind, and do not rest until your heart is established in the assurance of a personal union with your Heavenly Friend. Make up your mind entirely, as you have the most thorough warrant from Scripture for doing, that *He is your Friend*, and act accordingly. Cast all your care upon Him. Expect that there will be a great change in your heart, and in your life, but depend on Him to work it for you—to do it for you. You cannot fail—the arms of love are around you—of love everlasting. They must fail first.

SECTION III.

FRUITS OF GRACE.

THE RESPONSE OF THE SOUL IN VOLUNTARY SELF-SACRIFICE.

"For the love of Christ constraineth us; because we thus judge that if one died for all then were all dead: and that He died for all, that they which live, should not henceforth live unto themselves, but unto Him which died for them and rose again."—2 Corinthians v. 14.

* * * * * As to self-mortification distinguish always between that which is involuntary and that which is spontaneous. It is the latter upon which growth depends, and that is entirely the effect of faith.

* * * * * We often hear the phrase "clinging to the cross," meaning generally the cross of Christ, our only refuge from the fear of death. But is there not another much deeper meaning? When the fear of condemnation is entirely gone—gone through a view of the loving suffering One, and we are constrained to ask "What shall we render?" the answer comes: "Take up your cross and bear it for Him;" and we find in bearing it the strength we have long been praying for coming out of weakness—a fresh revelation of grace—a new development of life. O, how dear out own cross becomes; how we cling to it though it slays us, and because it slays us. We have wanted to be slain that we may truly live; that is the end and substance of our best prayers.

SECTION III.

FRUITS OF GRACE.

THE RESPONSE OF THE SOUL IN VOLUNTARY SELF-SACRIFICE.

I.

* * * * "THE joyful consciousness of entire devotion to God!" How blissful is even the hope of it, and how certainly your longing for it indicates that God Himself, by all His dealings, is leading you toward it—your crown.

Life, and the consciousness of life, a really entire devotion to God and the manifestation of it to the conscience, are two wholly distinct things. The first, the life, you have already, as certainly as any of those saintly persons whom you desire so much to resemble. A little more conflict with its earthly obstructions, chiefly with the legal element, and the seed long buried in dust will appear in all the beauty of the full-blown flower. To direct you and keep you steadfast in the preliminary struggle, is the end of all my endeavors. I shall have to be very *plain*, but for this you will be all the more grateful.

The whole difficulty in the way of God's fully manifesting His love to you, lies in the strength of your worldly desires. You half think that if you could be fully gratified on that point you would be permanently at rest. But, beside the doubt you have of its being attainable by all your efforts, there is another good you want still more, and the mere hope of which, if you knew certainly how to command it, would stop the pursuit of the other entirely. You want the love of Christ vastly more than you want the love of the world; but the very vastness of the bliss, combined with your sense of being so unworthy of it, makes you incredulous about attaining it. If you knew by what means you could give the higher good a clear ascendency, you would gladly avail yourself of them. Hence it is that you have rejoiced so greatly in the doctrine of faith, which gives so much more hope to your efforts. But you find that the doctrine cannot do everything, and you are taught, by a clear instinct, that there must be added to your faith "virtue," or a more vigorous self-denial. The great question on which your mind has been laboring for some time, is: What must I, what can I do in the way of self-denial?

And here is a point where an excited conscience, eclipsing for a time the light of faith, often leads to very serious mistakes, and, for a long time, to one struggling in a half-legal state, the whole subject seems a most complex one. One great mistake is, that we are apt to begin with a mere outward sacrifice, which conscience is demanding, but which faith will never allow. Speaking of the person whose life you have been reading with so much interest, you say, "she seemed to *begin* by first making a deliberate, solemn resolve to *surrender all.*" If that was really her beginning, depend upon it her resolve would have perished in its birth—in its early infancy, at any rate. There had been a preparation for that resolve. What at last brought it forth was the belief which had been, for a longer or shorter period, forming in her mind, as it is now in yours, that God's love and grace were such, and her sincerity, the effect of her belief in that love and grace, was such that she might at length make a resolve of that kind to an effectual purpose. She may have made the same, or thought of making it, often before; but now the spirit of the law had so far died within her by the same experience you are at present going through, the belief in God's love had become so rooted in her mind that she felt she might do what had long before been her great object of desire, as it is now of yours—that she might surrender herself so as to be joined to God in a perpetual consciousness of union. If she had done it under the legal notion that God required it as the condition upon which He would bestow something very valuable upon her, her subsequent experience would have been very different. Her sense of God's love and holiness had awakened the strongest desire to surrender herself to Him, and to enter into a perfect union with Him. She felt that nothing else could ever give her rest.

It was not that she was specially importunate for a manifestation of God's personal love to her, except (to use your own most appropriate expression) as "a power" by which she might be enabled to fulfill her whole duty to Him. At length, impelled by the strength of her desire to be entirely holy (entirely as far as it depends on the will), and the strength of her faith that God, of whose free and boundless love she had now a clear and firm conviction, could and would make her so, she truly surrendered herself; and though it was not intended as the *condition* of a manifestation from God, which had been the bane of all former attempts, that, after a few further struggles was the result, as it always must be. Her desire for holiness, and her faith in God's grace, growing together, had both become so strong, that she could not help doing everything she could that might forward the work of sanctification.

I cannot be mistaken in the belief that the same dispositions of faith and love are now growing in you, and advancing to the same result. Only two directions are necessary to ensure and hasten it. First, in every way head off legality, upon which I need say no more, as I have said so much; and, secondly, as far as you find yourself emptied of that element, and the love of God provoking the desire for holiness, be not timid or backward in your response. Be passive, as against legality, but with an earnest hope and expectation that the way will soon be clear for your becoming active. As far as it is clear, act now—live up to your freedom. Do not wait till your love is perfect, but let it work upward now, and according to its strength.

Beginning with the assurance that God certainly intends giving you a complete victory, (see Sixth Chapter of Romans,) let it be your determination, stronger every day, to wait upon Him, whatever your condition may be, until He fulfills His promise and purpose. Let this be the first exercise of your love—always first. If you can do nothing else, be determined to expect this result, fortifying your determination by all correspondent action, concluding at last, as you see there is no conscious insincerity to hinder, with giving yourself wholly to be the Lord's; and do not suppose that your sincerity is imperfect because you are conscious that sin exists in great power. Without this consciousness your sincerity would be proportionably imperfect.

It is because you feel that you never can conquer your sins while God is no nearer to you, that you desire a closer union with Him. And, depend upon it, that every effort you make to reach that union, though you see not your progress, is helping you towards it. Do not suppose that you will always have to struggle as you are now struggling. When God comes by that manifestation which, however it may be delayed, must come at last, it will strike sin in its very heart; you will know that you are its victor, and your relation to it, in your consciousness, will be just the reverse of what it is at present.

Only be guarded against the mistake of expecting this manifestation, and the sense of victory which it inspires, to commence at any marked era. It will probably come to your perception gradually, but the promise is, "exceeding abundantly above all that we can ask or think."

I believe I have nothing more to say to you at present, and shall probably not write to you hereafter except in application for counsel or sympathy, which, whenever made, I need not say it will be my greatest happiness to meet; for of all my earthly beatitudes there is none greater than I find in such ministrations.

II.

I CANNOT let a week pass, nor a day, without saying a few words in answer to your most affecting letter. I cannot rest an hour without telling you that your views of the nature of faith, as if you were, for a time, precluded from the most intensely joyful communion with Christ, are entirely erroneous.

You say, "I only want to know if this (trusting Christ) is all I am to do, or if not, what I am to do besides," etc.—that is, between depending simply on the promises and sympathy of the Saviour, which is faith alone, or upon these in connection with some "heart sacrifice" to appease a legal conscience, which is your old bane, your mind is still hesitating. You evidently have a doubt whether Christ does not require of you an "entire surrender" of some very dear thing before He will give you the pledge of His particular affection. Hence, while with one eye you are looking to Him, to His free grace, with the other you are looking at yourself to see that everything is right there also—that "conscience is not lulled"—that the sacrifice is real. You will not understand me that this state so far as expressed is not just as it should be. It is the state of the most thorough and simple believer—but it is the state also of the half-legalist and half-believer. The difference is, that the first, full of love to Christ because He has perfectly secured his salvation and left him nothing on that score to desire, cannot bear that anything offensive to such goodness should dwell within him, and is, therefore, ever watching his heart. The other, still uncertain of his salvation, because not knowing or believing that Christ has fully secured it, is the subject of a selfish anxiety to do the thing which may make it sure, and hence his concern about the "heart sacrifice."

His idea is, that Christ having revealed His love to the race in general, in order to make *himself sure* of it, in order to get a particular personal sense of it, something is required of him which will tax him not a little, and his great concern is to know what that thing is. He is afraid simple faith is not enough. Perhaps, besides this, there is something more to be done—some great heart-sacrifice.

How plainly can I see that the immediate end of all God's present dealings with you is to open your eyes through the pressure of your necessities to the *perfection of His love*—to the freeness and fullness of His salvation. What can I do for you but to tell you once more, yea, seventy times seven, of the unpurchasable love of Jesus!

Suppose it true that you are not willing to make the heart-sacrifice, or that you have doubts about it. Can you ever do it, while you look upon it as necessary to secure the love of Jesus, or any manifestation of that love to your soul? Suppose on the other hand that, in your present state, He does not ask it, but says, "My child, I know all your difficulties—I know what sore temptations mean—I have suffered them all, simply that I might know how to succor you, or rather that you might know how tender I can be. Now, give yourself in your present weakness no more trouble about sacrifices. Your sighs and groans under a sense of your deficiencies are more acceptable to Me than anything else you can now render, but a change is coming; you soon shall have such a sense of My love that nothing can be a sacrifice. Every blessing of salvation is yours now, if you would but give Me credit for what I have done for you. It is not a *state*, a something to be obtained by painful effort and seeking. Act upon that belief through all difficulties, and in a little while this truth will be perfectly plain to you." Will you not hear His voice, will you not trust Him?

You need not give yourself a moment's further concern about the nature of the self-denial which He will ask from you in the future. You will furnish the only sufficient test of the sincerity of your desire for Him at present, by enduring His long delays, because you have His word to sustain you. This *is* thorough self-denial. There is no trial like that which one suffers when all hope from the Law, that is, from such outward sacrifices as he is competent to, forsakes him, entirely forsakes him, and he sees that nothing can save him but simple Grace, and that this will not unless he submits to have his heart's heart, the very life of self, taken out of him. Thus give your whole self to Christ. Rest simply on the love of God as revealed in the Gospel, and as you do this, you will find, without mistake, that it is already all yours, and being persuaded of that, self and the world will have to relinquish their hold, and leave you free to give all to God. The change may not be, probably will not be, overwhelming, but it will be increasingly clear.

O, my Master and Lord, if even the heart of the

earthly helper was broken, and poured itself out to Thee in gratitude and grief, when he heard that the prayer of this soul has been for months, "O Saviour, reveal Thyself, reveal Thyself!"—in gratitude that this prayer was going up, and in grief for the soul still sorrowing, canst *Thou* long delay?

Be of good courage, the hour approaches when your Lord will come; an hour of darkness may intervene, but in that hour, and through it, you will learn His love and faithfulness.

III.

I FEEL that I have obtained, through my late conversation with you, a much clearer view of your position, including both your infirmities and your advantages, than I have ever had before. Perfectly persuaded, as I am, not only of the genuineness of your faith, but that I thoroughly understand the most interior causes of its weakness, nothing has restrained me from writing long ago, but the feeling that I could not compress my solution of your difficulties within any reasonable bounds, which, indeed, is no tax upon me; for of all earthly occupations there is none which gives me such pleasure as the endeavor to strengthen the weak,—but I have feared you might think it was a tax.

To relieve you, then, as much as possible, of all such feelings, let me first say, that an occasional letter of the kind I am about to write to you, is not only necessary as satisfying the longings of friendship, but nothing else is so important to keep up my spirit in the work with which I am at present mainly occupied. Writing to you seems like the pæan before sermon—a part of the same service.

I proceed, therefore, at once, first to take an observation for the purpose of determining exactly where you are in your course heavenward, and then to solve, if I may, some of the doubts and perplexities by which your aspirations are checked and your progress impeded.

You have always shrunk from the thought of dying to the world—of the heart's dying to those visions of beauty which fancy is ever painting on the cloud-curtain of the future. While you have felt it to be impossible by any mere energy of will to transfer yourself from the sensible to the spiritual, though convinced that the former is only an illusion, it has almost given you the life of which you were despairing, to learn that there was a way by which this transfer might be effected *for* you, despite your impotency; a way in which, without any action of your own but that of simple faith in the Divine promise, and of patience for a season like that of the husbandman who waiteth for the harvest, you would find yourself at length in such sensible communion with Heaven, that separation from the world you had loved so much would come at last almost without a sense of pain.

You cannot depend too confidently upon God's promises—be sure of that—His promises of justification, of sanctification, and of Heaven; but, for that very reason, in order to fulfill the great purpose of His love in making you a "partaker of His holiness," you may be just as certain of His providential corrections. The promises without the corrections, and the corrections without the promises, would be alike unavailing. By corrections I mean the thwarting of our worldly desires, especially at the point where we are most sensitive. It is all-important to remember that this is never done "willingly." "As a Father pitieth his children, so the Lord pitieth them that fear Him."

But though He afflicts not willingly, but for our profit, we may assume, for that reason, that He will do it firmly and thoroughly.

Suppose that, beside justifying us freely by His grace, and giving us a renewed assurance, from time to time, that His loving-kindness should never fail us, or that our salvation was perfectly secure—suppose he should give us, also, the very things which, in this world, we most coveted, preserving them, also, from corrupting on our hands, what would be the effect of such a course? If the only restraint upon the love of the world, in former days, was the fear of losing salvation, how unrestrained would it be now that the fear is wholly removed by the promise of justification, and every opportunity for enjoying the world is freely opened by a providential dispensation? How, in God's plan—God, whose ways of kindness are as much above ours as the heavens are above the earth—is this entire deliverance from fear, to which the Gospel gives the largest encouragement, and which, in so far as we are renewed, tends so mightily to holiness, prevented from becoming, through our remaining corruption, as mighty an occasion of license! Man's way, you know, is by a compromise of Law and Grace, making our final justification depend upon our good behavior, thus destroying the main incentive to good behavior. God's way is by providential corrections.

Nothing has been so memorable in my own life as the persistency with which Providence has thwarted my deeper worldly aspirations. Certainly for many years I have been in the habit of returning as heartfelt thanks for the discipline of God's Providence as for the love of His promises; so plain it is that I have been saved by the combination. Not in a moment, nor in a month, has this result been obtained—but I can truly say that in the wreck and ruin of worldly ambition and hope I have found a joy in comparison with which their highest realization would have been an empty shadow.

We must always remember, however, that such passages as these—"If any man would be the friend of the world he is the enemy of God;" "If any man love the world, the love of the Father is not in him;"—are not a prohibition of earthly affections, but only of putting them in the place of God. Enjoyed as the gifts of God, they are important means of promoting our union with

Him. It is only as His rivals that they are to be mortified. "Love not the world, neither the things of the world," is an injunction which it is impossible for creatures of our constitution to obey literally; or, if we could, it would be a constitutional imperfection. Our real virtue is in proportion to our susceptibility of receiving pleasure from them; for only to that extent can they be a temptation, and thus an index of the strength of a higher affection. We are taught in the Scriptures that the most intimate earthly relationships are the genuine types of that union with God, the only ideal of true happiness—the goal towards which all Christians are pressing.

> "What if earth
> Be but the shadow of heaven and things therein,
> Each to the other like more than on earth is thought."

Life is love, whether in the natural or the spiritual sphere; but fallen as we are from God, the shadow has taken the place of the substance. Hence the very peculiarity of his constitution which awakens in the Christian the desire for a personal union with God, based in the affections, creates incidentally the whole difficulty in reaching it. We find difficulty in everything, and often the greatest of all in things innocent of themselves, which prevent the current of the heart from flowing as fully and freely as it should towards its worthiest object.

That, in short, is a diseased state, in which the soul is secretly longing after any form of earthly good with the kind of interest with which it ought to cleave to God. We were made to find our happiness in the creature as well as the Creator; but in the former so subordinately that the exclusion of the heart from that source of pleasure should be no more felt than the loss of a rill by one who is conscious of possessing the fountain. How prone are we, knowing that God is more than willing that we should have every worldly happiness which is consistent with a supreme love to Him, under the pretext of a grateful appreciation of this kindness, to indulge ourselves in every natural desire, shunning, just as far as we can, with any conscience at all, the work of flesh mortification. How many of our thoughts, desires, and actions are an expression or manifestation of love to Him, and how many of them an expression of our love to the world? There is scarcely a day but throws some light on this question—

scarcely an act which does not indicate, more or less, the imperfection of our love to Him, and of our trust in His promises, and the strength of our love to the world and the things of the world.

I am not speaking of all Christians, but of those who have not yet clearly overcome the world, and are particularly sensible of its temptations. Even our religious duties, in many cases, are but attempts to lull the rebukes of conscience, that we may enjoy the world with less anxiety and more freedom. Even our prayers for complete sanctification, or a perfect victory over sin, are often more prompted by the love of ease, and an unwillingness to endure *for Christ's sake*, than by that growing love which cannot be satisfied with anything short of a perfect conformity to His will.

Open now the windows of the soul, and let in the most chastening, and at the same time the most cheering ray of Divine illumination which ever found entrance there. Your Divine friend is ever watching the movements of your heart with all the sensitiveness of the most devoted human friend. You can grieve Him by any indications of a doubtful or divided affection; you can melt

Him by signs of repentance; you can delight Him by peculiar demonstrations of sincerity. This sensitiveness is the charm of your relations to Him. Remember also, that while an earthly friend gives you his affection because he thinks you to be truly lovable, (Christ loves you because you are capable of becoming so,) though at present in His sight it may be as far from it as possible, and His purpose is to make you so accordingly. It is His persistency in forgiving and forgetting all your ingratitude and unfaithfulness, though He perfectly knows it, and it grieves Him sorely, that has chiefly endeared Him to you, as it ever will in the future; and it is your growing knowledge of His love, as so utterly unlike the love of man, that has at length begotten in you the desire, not so much for any change in His dispositions toward you, which you know are as good as they can be, as for a change in your dispositions and exhibitions toward Him.

Depend upon it that this susceptibility to the claims of Christ upon our supreme affection, though painfully conscious as yet of the power of rival affections, of which we would fain be delivered, is the kernel of the whole matter, the germ of a perfect sanctification. If the fountain which has been opened in the heart by "seeing the Son and believing on Him," can be kept open—kept living—though its streams at present scarcely flow, being obstructed by so many obstacles, a manifestation of God's love awaits the soul, than which there is nothing higher or greater for man. "In that day ye shall know that I am in my Father, and ye in me, and I in you."

IV.

WHEN I tell you that I have done nothing but write letters since I have recovered my writing faculty, you will understand why I have kept you at arm's length so long. I have many friends of from ten to thirty years' standing who are dependent upon me for a word of remembrance now and then, and of these, every one to whom I have been writing within the past month is in fresh sorrow.

Meanwhile, I have never been more anxious to communicate something to you than during these days which have been so filled up with attentions to others. There is no relaxation, nor ever can be, of my care for you. The more ground you gain, the greater is my ardor to help you to perfect victory. I see constantly a glorious crown before you, but I see always with equal clearness the conflicts through which you must reach it. These, however, I have rather kept out of view until you were perfected in the doctrine of Christ, the armor which makes us invincible. The object to which I have been almost exclusively confined has been to settle you in the belief that it is Christ's love to us, and not at all our love to Him on which the issue depends, and thus I have reasonably and scripturally hoped to beget in you that love to Him which would make you ready to take up those appointed crosses, when they should be presented in His Providence, which constitute the sure and direct way to the crown—meaning by the crown, in this sense, always, the consciousness of your high relationship to Him, which is all that we can reach in this world.

Long have I felt that the time had come when I should aim to make you more familiar with the personal Cross; but my tenderness has made me shrink from that strain as much as possible, while your experience and reflection have doubtless in a great measure supplied my lack in that service.

And here let me say that I want you to read a book which I will send to you to-day—Baldwin Brown's volume on the "Divine Life," the last chapter of which, called "The Way Home," you must consider as a letter from me, as furnishing just the Directory, or Itinerary, for Zion's pilgrims, which I have so long felt myself pressed to prepare for you. The book altogether is more elaborate than and superior to the "Exodus." The remarkable feature of the volume, indeed of both the volumes, is that they illustrate the connection between sin and sorrow (giving therein the most lucid view of the nature of sin), and the manner in which the one is used for the gradual destruction of the other, as no books that I know have done; in other words, the nature of the personal Cross, and the motives which enable us to bear it in their true connection. I trust it may furnish to you, as it has to me, a strong staff in weariness.

I wish I could make myself clear to you in my ideas of the way of "dying unto sin." I do not think I understand what you mean by "the danger of fastening our thoughts and energies on the dying," unless it is (and this I suppose it is) self-reflection. I must say, that with me this is much the most important part of the process; but let me explain: I do not mean by this a *deliberate habit* of self-reflection—for this habit itself has been induced (though it seems a paradox) by the confidence in which I have lived for years, and in which I am perfectly established, that all carefulness about our sanctification in the way of studied efforts for it, unless founded on an absolute assurance that it is already ours in Christ, will defeat itself; that we have nothing to do but to depend on Christ for it, as we depend on Him for justification. This absolute dependence on Christ, and, of course, corresponding love for Him, cannot but beget the desire for a closer and still closer union with Him, which we know nothing can hinder but some cherished, or at least overlooked, evil of heart or life. With such views how can one avoid self-reflection? Arising from such a principle self-reflection is one of the primary means of grace. A deep self-knowledge is one of the most fundamental distinctions between lower and higher degrees of grace—and this comes only by *enduring* the cross of self-reflection. I believe that this constitutes the essential cross of the Christian life, the aggregate of all its trials; outward afflictions being merely the accidents by which this is induced. Until the Christian knows, by the clearest intuition, that his union with God is perfect, he is alive with the apprehension that something is wrong, and to find out what that is, is the chief work.

There is nothing that I am so anxious about, that I pray for with such an agony, that I am so afraid of missing through my impatience of trial; or what is nearly the same thing, through the deceitfulness of sin, as this humbling view of my own corruption; and the chief reason why I so seek this before everything else is, that thus only am I compelled to (as you express it) "throw myself out of myself," "out of the dying into the living," if I apprehend your meaning in those expressions. The "living" is Christ's fullness, "the living bread which came down from Heaven;" the "dying" is my emptiness. I do not see that emptiness once for all, and ever after that spontaneously throw myself on the living Christ. That is what people sometimes think they are doing, when they are merely living on a former experience, or on a doctrine which a former experience has taught them. The hardest of all things in the Christian life is to avoid living in this way, by going deeper and deeper into the needs created by their ever active corruption, thus keeping up a perpetual hunger for some new manifestation, which, as Christ is true (the condition being their self-emptiness), shall be as perpetually satisfied.

The routine of living upon a doctrinal faith concerning Christ, instead of upon his living presence, is one of the chief impediments of Christian progress ; and this comes from not dying daily, or being willing to do so.

Have you ever doubted that Fenelon, Madame Guyon, and others like them, had as perfect a sense of their dependence upon Christ, and as simple a reliance upon His sacrifice for justification as we have, and yet have you not longed to know how it was that they attained to such a high measure of self-sacrifice, and of the service of God ?

Do not suppose that I think lightly of your self-knowledge, or that you are in particular danger of aversion to self-reflection. I have thought just the contrary. I want rather to encourage you in thus bearing your cross by the assurance that you shall yet reap from it the choicest fruit of the Christian life—fruit which can be reached in no other way. This dwelling in an element of suffering is one of the most clear and frequently expressed positions of the New Testament as essential to sanctification.

And yet, let me say that I consider the only healthy state of the soul that, in which it is so interested in the person and work of the Saviour, and in the character of God as therein manifested, as will render self-reflection for *any other purpose* but that of avoiding sin, and taking deeper draughts of God's grace as deeper depths of unworthiness discover themselves, almost unknown. Keep your eye fixed upon the one great Sacrifice, your Lord and Redeemer, and then will you pass through the furnace with a song rather than a plaint.

V.

I AM not content to *wish* you a happy New Year. As far as I can, I must do something to create what I wish. Earlier in our lives a happy New Year meant simply and solely the fulfillment, providentially, of some earthly aspiration, and to the end of mortal life none of us are wholly insensible, nor ought to be, to such outward favors. These I must be content to wish you, as I can do so little to insure them. I rejoice that your Father knoweth how far you have need of them, and how far you are better without them. But our common aspiration at present is to reach that point of spiritual development in which the earthly allotments once most importunately desired are felt to be outward indeed, feeling that neither their possession nor absence can affect our substantial happiness.

May I but be instrumental in keeping up your faith and hope to that ideal, and in materially aiding your progress towards it. What encouragement we have in the ground already gained! For myself, I am as happy as I can expect to be on earth. I am conscious that no New Year's day within my memory (and I have a very distinct remembrance of the past) has found me in such deep repose as I enjoy at present. The radical fact is, that the Divine life within me has outgrown and overcome my strongest natural proclivities, which, I am sure, were never stronger in any one. I am no longer doubtful of my heavenly inheritance, for the foretaste of it here is a perfect antidote to the feverish agitations of earthly passions.

It was not so but a short time ago, which, with all above that relates to my own experience, I mention for your encouragement, rejoicing, also, to magnify the Lord's loving-kindness, and His promises of grace. "I have not hid Thy righteousness within my heart; I have declared Thy faithfulness and Thy salvation."

I believe you can give something of the same report, notwithstanding your remark, last summer, that you "had not grown any in two years"—that is, there had not been much alteration in your consciousness during that time. But you have found the Pearl, and now I want to show you how you may and will come to a more full and perfect consciousness of its use and value.

In the childhood of the Christian life we can bear but little. Nature (in ordinary conditions of prosperity) is too exacting, and the world too dear to us to allow those inward sacrifices which are the necessary condition of a life of holiness. God deals with us as with children—taking care to prevent our being over-tempted by too much worldly indulgence on the one hand, and by too little on the other. We must grow by degrees to a certain capacity for spiritual sacrifices (though some grow much faster than others)—to a state in which they shall be spontaneous, or no sacrifices really, before they are imperatively demanded, or before their necessity to our progress in grace is a matter of clear revelation.

We grow to this capacity by a thorough trial of the Divine forbearance, gentleness, and goodness. As we become able to trust, we become disposed to venture, and ashamed of our former inaction. The privilege of giving, by which I mean of spontaneous inward sacrifice, for which we once felt ourselves unable, becomes as dear as that of receiving without the giving had been before. There is a new tendency in this direction, and very certainly, it is just in so far as this tendency is encouraged and becomes a fixed habit, just in so far as we actually give up everything else for the sake of Christ, do we experience that personal communion with Him which is the object of our best aspirations.

You know how in human cases, the knowledge that one of our own kind suffers, and suffers gladly out of love to us, how it draws our hearts to him so that we refuse nothing that we can give. Can you doubt, my dear child, that Christ is looking upon you just in the same way? For the smallest of your real sacrifices for Him He is preparing for you an immortal crown. The whole reason of His not communicating Himself in all His beauty to your consciousness at once is, that thus He would deprive you of the opportunity of manifesting your love to Him in the only way in which it can be manifested here, by endurance for His sake, and thus of inheriting a larger reward.

For some years past God has been teaching you His lovableness, and His desire for your love. It has had a great effect upon you; it has been gradually drawing your heart to Him. You have not been wanting in a high degree of responsive action—let that action now be complete. Take it for granted that He, and all He can give, are yours, already yours, and draw from this immeasurable wealth the motive and the power to give yourself wholly to Him—wholly.

It gives me the highest pleasure that I can send you such a book as Goulburn's "Thoughts on

Personal Religion." It is only within a few days that I have read a page of it, but there are parts of it, (see Chapter III., Part 1) which have moved me as Peter's Pentecostal sermon did the three thousand, owing partly, perhaps, to a peculiar personal preparation for it. How much depends upon the preparation of a sensitive conscience, and a thirsty heart, to get from such books all that they are able to give!

And now, my dear friend, in looking back upon the past years of our pilgrimage, can we not at least say that this New Year finds us in the enjoyment of a far stronger sense of the reality of the love of Christ than we once had,—of its all-sufficiency for the happiness of the soul without any addition from earth? Not, perhaps, that we have no earthly longings left, but are they not much reduced by the much stronger belief than we once had of the good which there is in Christ,—of His intimate relations with the soul,—more intimate infinitely than those of our nearest kindred; of His love so much sweeter in its nature, to say nothing of its depth and breadth? And yet, in another sense, our love to Him makes our affection for each other far deeper than it could otherwise be; indeed, gives it its immortal meaning.

I can only say, that loving you, as I do, in Him, I know my love for you can never die. Many of my friendships prove but blossoms, which the winds of time scatter; but our friendship formed in the "bud of our being," shall have the growth of eternity. How overwhelming the thought that you and I who have talked so much together of the hidden life and of the Saviour, while knowing Him only by faith, shall resume our communion upon these subjects after that life shall have been fully developed by the sight of Him in glory.

VI.

I HAVE too much faith in your generosity to fear that you ever attribute the long intervals which sometimes come between my letters to any intermission of interest. You know from long experience that my interest in you is ever green; flourishing alike in summer heats and in winter frosts. My mind is habitually burdened with thoughts which might perhaps somewhat relieve you in your inward and outward struggles.

But there are times when my conscience binds me to allow as few interruptions as possible to my public vocation, and the more stringently as the time in which I have to work dwindles into a narrower space. It is some comfort to think that what I feel for you is never unnoticed above, and may be doing more for you there than any or everything I could say to you here. It is a great satisfaction to be assured from the general tone of your letters, that you are so submissive to your trials, and yet so aspiring still; so thankful for your common blessings, however alloyed with disappointment, and so trustful even for the higher which are promised. The Divine labor upon you has not been wasted. I join with you in praising Him for the "hunger and thirst" which you "know" you have; and though you dare not think yourself quite ready yet for an entire self-sacrifice, I am well satisfied for the present that you can say "I want to be." I am hardly more certain of the Gospel itself than I am that all its beatitudes are already germinally yours. For their more rapid development into blossom and fruit, my spirit is habitually bowed in supplication in your behalf.

I wish particularly in this letter to convey my idea of the position in which you now stand toward the object of your aspirations, and of what you may do yourself to further the work which God most certainly is working in you. The main point to which you should be constantly pressing forward is a more entire self-sacrifice, about the nature of which your ideas are generally right, and yet they require to be made more definite. Self-sacrifice (essentially) is the offering of the soul unto God, which is made by the Christian daily in his prayers. In "the saint made perfect," in whom self as an opponent of God is entirely destroyed, such an offering is attended with no *sacrifice*. This is predicable only of the saint in whom the love of God—the principle of the new creature—is still but a germ, growing side by side with an evil heart of unbelief which acts as a constant obstruction even to its gradual development.

A never intermitted suggestion of this heart of unbelief is, that the only self-devotion upon which God looks with complacency is that which is impossible, except to a high degree of purity, when the heart, entirely loosed from its selfish fetters, bounds upward spontaneously, as by a law of gravitation.

Suppose this were true, where would be the sacrifice? Certainly, to reach such a state is the end and aim of all our efforts; and it is equally true that until there is an element of spontaneity in our offerings, such a state can hardly be an object of aspiration. But it is by a succession of just such difficult and imperfect efforts that we gradually approximate our end.

There are no saints on earth who are not more sensible of their sin than of their holiness; for although a decided progress in the Christian life cannot but be marked (I should think) by some consciousness of increasing holiness, yet a still more certain sign of it—a more common, and equally certain at least—is a sharpened sense of the evil which still dwells within. I question whether any one ever attains a higher sanctification on earth than is expressed in your declaration, with the fullness of meaning that it might cover, "I want to be," or in the apostolic phrase, "to will is present with me,") a phrase which perfectly describes the state of the regenerate up to the moment of sin's final destruction.

The difference in degrees in sanctification is simply the difference in the intensity or strength of the "will," of this sense of want. In Christians of a low degree, or under peculiar temptations, the "will" or "want" to be holy may be too feeble even to identify its subject as a Christian, though it may have an obscure existence. In another, it may be so strenuous as to sweep all before it, to an outside view; and yet it is certain that what distinguishes the latter from the former quite as much as anything else, is his far quicker sense of the strength and subtlety of indwelling sin. While his "want to be" holy is hardly less than perfect, his sense of another counteracting will or want is just as strong. It is this sense of a body of sin, cleaving to his most vital powers, ever deepening as he advances in the knowledge of God, which gives depth and intensity to his daily prayers, or prompts him to even intenser efforts of self-sacrifice.

Smitten with a sense of Divine love, and yet oppressed with the difficulty of making a proper return for it through the power of remaining corruption, the prayer of a true saint (in his better states at least) is mainly an effort to expose this corruption to the burning judgment of the All-Holy and Omniscient eye, and to hold it there until it is consumed by the brightness of the revelation which the Gospel affords.

This is my idea of the essential nature of that self-sacrifice which constitutes or should constitute the daily habit of the Christian. It supposes a strong desire for holiness, and as strong a sense of its absence. But can you suppose that such efforts as these will be without effect, or that the effect will always be so inward as to be invisible? that the bitter bud will never burst into a fragrant flower? The time may seem long, but the result is as certain as that God lives and loves. The truth is, it is all the while bursting into such a flower, "a sacrifice of sweet savor unto the God of Heaven;" and with every such sacrifice on our part there is a nearer approach to us on God's part.

You will experience the consuming revelation exactly as you make the sacrifice it demands. It does not come as a flash of lightning, at once and forever dissolving our bonds of sin, but as the gray dawn revealing for a good while more darkness than light, and urging us onward as much by the fear of losing, as by the expectation of enjoying, the perfect day. All that remains then is that you gird yourself for a more perfect self-sacrifice. You must guard against the idea that nothing can be done for the expulsion of sinful affections until the new and heavenly one has been fully matured. It is only by determined conflict that the latter gets its strength to expel the other. Remember, that though your affections were given you to enjoy the creature as well as the Creator, there is no creature enjoyment which is legitimate until you have first been given wholly and absolutely to God. All your enjoyment of earthly good in the past, or in your dreams of the future, however spuriously defended, this condition being unfulfilled, has been simply a robbery of God.

If Christ in the desert had said, "How can I do without bread?" or, "Surely I may possess the kingdoms of the world, and then use all My power over them for God's glory," the devil would have conquered Him. God has brought you into a desert; there are certain things which are peculiarly adapted to give you happiness, which you very much want; you do not yet see why they should be denied you. I will tell you why—*God is all-sufficient.* Acknowledge this by an absolute heart-sacrifice of everything else, and you will then receive the whole blessedness for which your nature was made.

And to help you still further, if I may, let me say a word about the nature of the blessing you will receive. The view which it was my special design to give you when I commenced this letter—a view which has given me an almost heavenly repose—is this: the highest point of progress, I apprehend, whatever experiences may grow out of it, which is ever attained in this life, is an established assurance that God is ours, that we never can be separated, and that our souls shall be ever getting nearer to Him.

Suppose you believed with as much certainty as you believe the Gospel to be true, that, unfaithful and unfruitful as you have been, God's purpose to purify and make you perfect in holiness, and thus perfect in happiness, would never change; all your allotments in life, and especially the most painful, even to the minutest circumstance of your history, being a part of His plan of grace, and as exactly fitted to its end as the various parts of a machine to the purpose of its designer—could you desire anything more than to live in such a faith continually? What a fund of joy such a faith would supply to you in all circumstances, and how it would prepare you for every sacrifice! Well, what hinders such a faith? Nothing is wanted but a perfect assurance that *God is Love.* You need no special personal assurance. From God's nature, of which the chief manifestation is the gift of His Son, it cannot be otherwise. Once become "rooted and grounded" in this blessed truth, and, of all the desires of your bosom, the dominant one will be that the sacrifice may be complete, entire, and thorough. You will rejoice, I might say, in the Divine jealousy; you will feel it to be the truest expression of Divine love. You will welcome its consuming operation as the means of coming to your highest joy. You will yield yourself up to trials with the ardor of a martyr who feels that through the stake he shall reach his blessedness, and in a little while you will realize your idea of self-sacrifice in all its purity.

I trust that I have not interfered with God's

work in your soul by prescriptions derived from my own experience which may contract the ground of your hopes, or by premature requisitions which, though they must come at last, may be too much for your present strength to bear.

Ever praying the Source of all love to hold you up "till your unwearied feet arrive where perfect pleasure is,' I remain, your friend.

SECTION IV.

TRIUMPHS OF GRACE.

THE SOUL'S CONQUEST OVER SIN, GROWTH IN HOLINESS, AND FINAL PERFECTION IN GLORY.

"BUT of Him are ye in Christ Jesus, who of God is made unto us wisdom and righteousness and sanctification and redemption." —1 Corinthians i. 30.

* * * * * A simple and determined and persevering faith in the doctrines of grace will certainly carry us to the heights of holy living. Justification by faith in Christ's vicarious righteousness is in its inward specific operation the principle or source of all personal holiness—is essentially the sanctification of believers —is the death of sin. * * * * * I am entirely convinced that the way in which we commonly seek sanctification, making holiness the basis of assurance, instead of assurance the basis of holiness, is directly opposed to the wisdom of God in the plan of salvation. The Bible here is at variance with our best philosophies.

"And whom He justified them He also glorified."—Romans viii. 30.

"That in the ages to come He might show the exceeding riches of His grace in His kindness towards us, through Christ Jesus."—Ephesians ii. 7.

* * * * * But who am I, that in me the assurance of the heavenly inheritance should not be presumption? There is nothing to make such assurance presumptuous but the guilt of sin —our desert of penalty in the place of reward. What means this passage, 'For He hath made Him to be sin for us who knew no sin; that we might be made the righteousness of God in Him?' Not to appropriate Heaven is not to believe in Christ. In believing in Christ and rejoicing with a joy full of glory even amidst all life's uncertainties and sorrows, and in assuming my final exaltation, I am honoring Him as I can do in no other way.

SECTION IV.

TRIUMPHS OF GRACE.

THE SOUL'S CONQUEST OVER SIN, PROGRESS IN HOLINESS, AND FINAL PERFECTION IN GLORY.

I.

IN my last letter to you I promised another very soon, in which I proposed to answer the great question, "What shall I do?" which continues to agitate you. The general answer to this question is, that you must do just what you did in your first coming to Christ, only in a deeper manner, corresponding to the increased depth of your legal apprehensions. What the soul receives in its conversion will always correspond in kind with the desires by which it has been previously exercised, and in measure with the depth of its previous sufferings, and so ever afterwards.

What the soul generally desires in its earliest convictions is little more, if anything, than a sense of deliverance from the Law's penalty—a state of justification. From the gratitude thus awakened, from a desire to keep the liberty which it has found, and from some sense of the beauty of holiness (for there must be a germ of this nature in every case of real conversion), it then begins a struggle for sanctification—for that higher kind or less fluctuating form of peace and freedom which flows from a conscious union with God by love as well as by faith. This brings it often into a far deeper conflict than it knew before, in the course of which, in some cases, it is scarcely possible to avoid the most serious doubts whether it has ever been regenerated or justified at all—so serious, that at length, instead of being a contest for sanctification directly, it becomes a repetition only, in a deeper way, of the first struggle for life itself—for a state of justification—for a sense of God's paternal favor. And hence the very same process by which that blessing was first received must now be gone through with again, only in a deeper way, to recover and establish it.

Undoubtedly there are several respects in which your case differs very much from that of one who has never hoped at all in the Divine mercy. Any danger from the Law's last penalty perhaps hardly crosses your thoughts. But for the very reason that you think you have found deliverance from that, it the more confounds you that your heart is left to famish. If God is your God, why does He thus deal with you? Why does He keep so reserved? Why does He so hide His face from you? Why, while others can hardly find language to express their joys, are you denied that constant and delightful communion with Him, for the want of which your affections are ever wandering after earthly vanities, or only restrained from it by the fear of a still deeper anger?

You have been brought to see very clearly that the only real remedy for your wounded spirit is sanctification—that anything short of a great change in your *ruling affection* will do but little for the establishment of your peace; and though you are not conscious of that mighty desire for holiness which springs from its actual enjoyment, or from the force of love; yet as giving you a perfect sense of your justification, as a means of conquering all the enemies of your peace, and of fixing you in a state of unchanging fellowship with God you do desire it as you desire nothing beside. Assured at length that this, like every other blessing of salvation, is contained in Christ's infinite fullness, and derived thence by the simple process of believing, you want to do just what you did when you gained your first hope—come to Christ, trust in Christ, receive from Christ—always remembering that His love to you, not yours to Him in the slightest degree, must be your whole dependence—in the beginning of your Christian life, in all stages of its progress, and at its end. * * * * * The spring of the Divine life in the soul is a desire towards God, based originally upon a sense of his perfection, but called into immediate and lively action by the expression of His peculiar affection for us. The measure of our inward life will always correspond to the degree in which we are sensible of His *favor;* a sense of this such as we never had before, though it may still be comparatively faint, always marks the era of our conversion. It is an intimation, or what is so considered of God's love to us, which first awakens the sentiment of love to Him. It is then that in Him whom we have hitherto regarded only as our judge we begin to recognize the love of a Father, and in this love we find for a time our supreme felicity. Of course, how to retain this love, how to entitle ourselves to a fuller expression of it, how this new-born happiness may be enlarged and perpetuated, becomes the object of our chief solicitude. We feel that nothing can assure us of this but a life of holiness, meaning by this a life in which the love of God is perpetually triumphant over the love of the world. But we too often find that while conscience is strongly on the side of God, and not without a better feeling also arising from a sense of His kindness and generosity, (the will under this two-fold pressure making a constant and often a most earnest effort to be faithful,) yet some of our liveliest affections are still so much in the interest of the world that little or nothing comes of all our endeavors. We make no advance. We often question whether the heart's union with God which we hoped would soon be perfect is even begun. We become despondent of our ability even to attain a life of holiness. If we do not yield wholly to the tempter, we wage but a feeble conflict; our prayers, which ought to be full of confidence, being chiefly confessions of shame and deprecations of Divine judgment.

I cannot conceive that any dread of a hereafter, or the considerations which are addressed to conscience merely, powerful as these considerations are to awaken attention, are ever sufficient to conquer the love of the world. Nor can I conceive that any sense of the Divine authority and perfection, unaccompanied by a special tender of His love to us, and a promise of the most endearing and intimate personal fellowship could do it. The love of God, which repels all rival affections, springs not primarily from a sense of His perfection, however that may command our esteem and reverence, but from a belief or sense of His *infinite affection.*

The fullness of the love of God is manifested to us; attracts and moves us in the personality of Christ, our Saviour, so worthy of supreme love. Love in us is, at bottom, that response of the heart to which we are moved by a sense of the adaptation of such condescension to our helpless necessities.

"Ah," but you say, "the great proof of love to Christ is, that we keep his commandments, and herein I am conscious of a signal deficiency. I have no evidence of this sort upon which I can rely for a moment!" But the "keeping" of the commandments to which Christ promises His love and blessing is primarily that posture of believing-loving, or loving-believing attention and regard to His words which is produced by the dependence of our hearts upon him. It is the sighing to be more conformed to him. It is that repenting, coming, praying, hoping, believing, waiting, which His promises have inspired. These are pre-eminently, and first of all, His commandments. The *desire* to "keep" avails in the sight of grace, as if it were the full performance. For such as would fain love and keep, in the fullest sense, but cannot for the want of further strength—theirs is the blessedness of that hunger which shall certainly be filled; of those beginnings of purity which shall soon be perfected by the vision of God. Come, then, and take a fresh, life-giving draught of the love of Christ, just as when you first came to Him, only deeper and fuller, as your necessities are greater.

If Christ commands, He gives in the command itself the power of fulfilling it. Thus He commands us to love. Love is the essence and end of all His commands; but it is that love of which faith (faith in *His* love) is the root. The whole commandment, then, is not love alone, but faith also, which gives the power to love. If love is the end of the commandment, as Paul says (1 Tim., i. 5), faith is its beginning; not in the order of time, but in the order of nature. There is always just as much love as there is faith.

As faith grows into a habit of depending, leaning upon Christ's bosom and finding His succor in all your trials, love will grow in the same ratio, until at length not only will the easier sayings of Christ be fulfilled in your heart, but there will come an increasing inward demand for self-sacrifice, and a growing consciousness of the Divine complacency; for what you really want is His love of complacency, not alone the love of compassion, not merely "you in Him," which is equivalent to a sense of justification, but above all "Him in you," which is equivalent to sanctification. I am a firm believer in the omnipotence of *love!*

II.

I AM convinced by the letter just received that you are the subject of Divine instructions, and that much officiousness on my part would not promote the work of grace in your soul. But as a dear friend in Christ, I feel a deep pleasure in communion with you, and therefore readily embrace the opportunity for this, afforded by your letters. While we should not despise human instruction, I hope we shall not rest in it. It has the same relation to the work within, that the scaffolding has to a building itself.

I would guard you, especially, against leaning too much upon any human descriptions of sanctification. I find that this is a matter of experience, and that it has not been promoted in me by those exact representations of its nature which have led me to anticipate much about it. It is enough to know that our privileges vastly exceed our common thoughts of them, and that God can give us abundantly above all that we can ask or think. For myself I regard sanctification as a gradual work to the end of life, and I never expect to be able to say, I am now perfectly sanctified. You will inquire, however, "Is there not some special mark which you are in the habit of pursuing yourself, and of holding forth to others, under the name of Rest, which may be obtained by dwellers in the flesh?" There is,—and I believe, my dear friend, you know what it is by some experience, though that experience may not yet be complete. I mean by this, what the Apostle calls the full assurance of hope, and which he exhorts us to give all diligence to attain. The same thing is expressed by the Apostle when he prays for the Ephesians that "Christ may dwell in their hearts by faith;" and again, when he speaks of himself, as "walking by faith and not by sight." "If ye continue in the faith, grounded and settled, and be not moved away from the hope of the Gospel, which you have heard." "For we are made partakers with Christ if we hold the beginning of our confidence steadfast unto the end." But you may still ask, what is the specific nature of assurance, and how is it to be obtained? I answer, faith is assurance (as far as it goes). Assurance is nothing more than faith made strong by trial—or by an unremitted adherence to Christ in a great variety of circumstances. I much suspect that kind of assurance which is attended with an abrupt transition from some previous state—which is based on some strongly-marked, and sudden internal change, which admits no further improvement. Understand me—I believe such exercises are experienced by many Christians, and I greatly value them as helps to the attainment of assurance; but I think I know some whose experience in this way has been perverted to the nourishment of self-confidence, and others, whose eagerness for enjoyment of this kind forms the greatest hindrance to their attainment of assurance. I suppose assurance to be that state in which a Christian can hold on his way, however grievously his faith may be tried, because he is so confident of his foundation. It seems to me that just here is one great cause of your perplexity—you question your foundation. You talk about going forward to occupy "higher ground." You are mistaken. You never can get upon higher ground in this world than that on which you now stand. What you want is simply to be *rooted* and *settled* in your present state—to be assured that you need nothing in addition. I do indeed admit the necessity of advancing—that is, of growing upward, and outward, in the fruits of holiness; but I say further, that this will follow of itself from your growing downward in the principle of faith, and in no other way. This is the root of the tree. Graces, duties, and enjoyments, are the leaves—the flowers—the fruit—which will certainly appear in their season, provided the proper care be taken of the root. This then is the blessing to be directly sought after—a perfect union with Christ—a settled, rooted, unchanging confidence in Him—a habit of turning to Him momently as the needle to the pole. Thus, assurance will be ever growing. All your care must be given to cleaving to the vine. "As the branch cannot bear fruit of itself except it abide in the vine, no more can ye except ye abide in me." These are Christ's own words. Our growth must all be a work of faith—not of self-devised and self-directed effort for a blessing that is at best uncertain, but a cheerful and humble acquiescence in a Divinely-ordained method for obtaining a blessing already promised and purchased, and therefore, sure.

Let us renew our faith from day to day, by meditation, not upon ourselves, our infirmities, our unfaithfulness, but upon our all-sufficient Saviour, His person, character, and offices. Let every temptation to distrust, especially those arising from our sins, lead us to bring our spirits to Him in all their nakedness, to be clothed with a righteousness of His providing. Most certain I am that nothing but the thorough conviction which has been wrought in me by my life-failure, of the impossibility (in my case certainly) of an inherent righteousness which can give me boldness in death, could have so settled me in the doctrine of justification, and sanctification by Grace alone.

I may say that all my religious life has been an effort to get upon the ground—the rock—which I have at length reached. I had an early glimpse of it, as the Israelites had of a rest in Canaan, and everything else which a Christian, and especially a Christian minister, might set before himself as an object of desire has had but a small interest for me in comparison with this spiritual attainment. Growth in theological knowledge, and in public influence, have never occupied my heart. Growth in faith and love, terminating in a perfect consciousness of union with the Divine, and thus a perfect victory over the world (which has always had the strongest attractions for me), this is the only thing I have really coveted. The desire for more nearness to God, or for a higher purity, can no more be resisted than the impulse to breathe. I hope soon to see you, and to find you bounding like a deer in the Lord's pastures.

III.

My skies are clear! clear beyond all former precedent. The reading of Olshausen on Romans once more, in connection with recent experiences, has raised my faith to the highest point, I think, it has ever known. My soul has almost broken for the longing it has had to communicate my feelings, or rather my faith, to you.

Two things I should like to talk with you about could I give my thoughts utterance. First, What *is* this thing called sanctification—this thing for which so many of us so long and pertinaciously, and yet (with reference to the end as well as the way) so blindly struggle? Is it anything less than the *life of God in the soul?*—not merely the life which God gives, but the life which God *lives*—the Divine life, "and all that life is Love!" Can I say more?

Secondly, How is it attained? Hear Olshausen: "According to Paul's way of thinking, the blessedness of the man is certain only because God has promised it, and certainly intends it, and he only who believes in this decided will of God has this salvation wrought in him.

"It now becomes clear how faith is one and all in the Christian life. The Christian has neither before nor after his conversion to generate an independent sanctification of his own, but he has only constantly to receive the stream of the influential powers of Christian life upon him, and this receiving is faith itself. Just as the tree, when the development of its germ is begun, has only to suck in water, air, and light, in order to unfold itself from within, and all the drawing of a stupid gardener at the branches, all his working at the buds to coax forth blossoms, can only disturb but never further its development."

Have we not a higher witness to this truth than Olshausen? But how strongly do his words confirm within us the truth of the things which we already believe, and by the faith of which we live. About Olshausen, I have only further to say that his commentary on John interests me nearly in the same degree as his Romans. You shall have them both, together with Müller on the "Christian Doctrine of Sin," which I am reading with great interest and wonder, and with very great profit.

Have I told you how the controversy concerning the nature of the Atonement, as conducted by Young in his "Christ, the Life and Light of Men," shook me to my very soul's center? I happened to read it at a time when spiritual disease within me appeared, as never before, hopelessly chronic; when I was only sustained by the belief that it was not the malady alone which caused my pain and weakness, but the Divine surgery which was working to heal me. But what tortured me was the temporary eclipse of faith, the possibility of a mistake as to the efficacious nature of the Atonement, compelling me to look more closely at the amount of my (graciously received) inherent personal righteousness, and what might be expected from it. But never did I have so wholesome a discipline. While it brought into strong relief the root of all evil in my heart, it revealed at the same time the formal, traditional, superstitious character of much of my faith—the faith on which I had depended to cover the evil. How little should we ever know the depths of deceit within us, but for such trials; and how hopeless the effort to rise to a full appreciation of the things above, while ignorant and unconscious of the dark ruin within, out of which we shall at last see that by the merest grace, God's inheritance in the saints is constructed.

Under the new, purified assurance which has resulted from these trials my mind is now in full action, reasoning some, rhapsodizing some. I do not see how it is possible that I ever can be satisfied with an Atonement which does not contain a thorough antidote to the sense of guilt. It is, I think, the instinctive and ineradicable belief of men that the principle which constrains God to punish is as essential to His righteousness as that which constrains Him to love; and what makes that love and its consequences in Redemption the theme of highest, holiest rapture, is, that it had, by some means, to reconcile with it another principle, which was just as essential to Divine perfection.

Upon my mind the fact of an Atonement in the sense of a satisfaction to justice is fixed more firmly than ever. I cannot see why it was necessary that God should become man merely to induce reconciliation on man's part, by a revelation of God's nature. I admit such revelation is the greatest *means* of reconciliation on man's part; but if that were all, or the main thing to be accomplished by the Incarnation, I cannot but feel that the means were wholly out of proportion to the end. But if before He could institute any policy in our favor, or make any revelation for our good, it was necessary that eternal justice should be vindicated in such action to itself—if, in other words, an eternal necessity in the Divine nature required a vicarious sacrifice, corresponding to infinite holiness, and the infinite ill-desert of sin, that adequately explains the necessity of the Incarnation. *How* this reconciliation was brought about by the Incarnation and suffering of the Son of God is a mystery; and all those fail who try to solve it to the understanding. Some, in attempting it, de-humanize God; others un-deify Him. Philosophy is incomplete to sound these depths. "I love the incarnate mystery."

And now, in defining my belief as to what you and I may reach in the way of communications from Christ, and service to Him, I should say, it is that we may hope to attain what we call sanctification in this life, not in the sense of being free from every motion of sin, or from occasional lapses, it may be, by reason of sudden surprisals co-operating with remaining weakness; but in the sense of being purified from every *principle* of sin, from every way of sin; so that we may have the abiding consciousness of serving Christ with our whole hearts, and have a constant and serene (though by no means ecstatic) confidence of His love to us—love which shall keep up a joyful sunshine within, however we may be tried externally. This was certainly a common state among the primitive Christians, and is but the natural effect of a simple faith in the Gospel doctrines. A simple, and determined, and persevering faith in these doctrines will certainly carry us to the heights of holy living.

As to what I mean by a *simple* faith, I would explain thus—though not without some exercise of heart upon these Gospel doctrines, or, which is the same thing, some endeavor to appropriate their living virtue—is there not much danger that in our profession as ministers we shall be influenced by the same motives, in studying them, and in presenting them to others, which ordinarily prompt to the study of the natural sciences?—that is, that the exercise of the intellect, in the endeavor to give them a philosophical form, or an original expression, rather than to *apply* them in all the spirituality of their meaning, will absorb us too much; and does not this have a manifest tendency to destroy the simplicity of Christian doctrines, and make them unfit for our inward life? Have we anything to do, but for ourselves to appropriate, and for the people to whom we preach to apply these life-giving truths? Let us pray more earnestly for power to preach the Gospel—for power to prevail in this matter against self, and against Satan. Why should not the continuance of faith and prayer work a perpetual deliverance from that principle of self-regard which causes so much of our misery, and of our want of success—we may say, the whole of it? What we want is that the power of Satan over us (as God's servants) may be terminated by such a clear, abiding consciousness of the identity of our personal interests with the prosperity of Christ's kingdom as will divest our cares entirely of their selfish form, and make them cares only for His honor. Thus, let us trust unreservedly to the power of prayer, casting away every other defense.

God is near you, my brother, and He will ever be drawing nearer, nearer, nearer.

IV.

* * * * * * "RELIEF of the heart"—yes, this is what you want. Relief of the heart, not merely through the manifested love of some superior Being, but through the consciousness of some relation to Him which gives you a legitimate claim to it. You want to have the consciousness that you are giving your Heavenly Friend the same satisfaction in kind, however less in degree, which the sense of His love imparts to you. This is my ideal of the inward life of a Christian. A long and troublous experience has made it certain to me that the higher consequences of Christ's Divine Humanity are but poorly developed in most of our Protestant schemes. They may be contained in them, and doubtless are, but they have not been distinctly, fully, and vividly developed. The Atonement of Christ, which satisfies the conscience, needs to be supplemented by as peculiar a doctrine respecting the Person of Christ, which alone can satisfy the soul. It is true that latterly we hear much more of this in the preaching of the day, and in many of the books; and the eagerness with which such views of Christ are received, show the deep want which they meet.

The Roman Catholic Church, the refined portion of it, had a right conception of this doctrine, as you may see in Tauler and Thomas à Kempis; but its benefits were soon lost to the multitudes through a corruption not so much doctrinal as practical, which virtually precluded all rest to the conscience, and therefore to the heart.

Conscience must be entirely free, in a way glorious to God's justice—works must be utterly excluded before a true and sincere heart-relation with God can begin. Without this, the subjective sentiment in man becomes a vigorous self-righteousness, more or less sublimated, which represents the Roman Catholic corruption, or that polished, speculative, ineffectual nonentity which represents the Socinian.

It is not, therefore, without the highest reason that the Protestants have made the doctrine of a vicarious satisfaction to justice, and its practical consequence, justification by faith alone, their great bulwark of defense. You said nothing to me in your letter about the "History of Port Royal." How did you like it? I trust it has done you no harm—of which, however, I am not so certain, considering its strong legal and ascetic tendency.

Nevertheless the grandest and most elevating sentiment, to me, of Christianity, is recognized in the monastic system—the sentiment that Christ is the true and proper Bridegroom of the soul. Certainly it was the influence of that sentiment which drove so many both of the strong and the lovely to seek in the cloister a shelter from the world's contamination. It was devotion to the unseen Lover of the soul, though a superstitious and irrational devotion, which forbade them to find joy in anything but spiritual intercourse. I do not suppose that this was the common motive, but that it was so in many cases. I do not admire the institution, nor regret that we have nothing in Protestantism that corresponds with it. It is condemned alike by reason and Scripture; it was the natural product of an age of ignorance and licentiousness, and its best practical effect was to bind the conscience without at all relieving the heart.

I have been thinking a great deal about this subject of late, as I told you in my last letter, and, with the hope of meeting, possibly, some of the wants of the heart, I have been writing a sermon, in which, in brief, I show that the original relationship of the soul to God was a love relation.

Through temptation the soul has fallen into the same relation to the world which it was made to hold to God, and which it once actually held to Him. It seeks its happiness in the world. But not finding it there—having more or less of disappointment—it seeks to return. But, in doing so, it meets all those difficulties which arise from the *law relation* (the Divine justice and holiness), which make a reunion morally impossible. Christ appears, and by the great work of the Atonement puts all these law difficulties (which are the only difficulties) out of the way. There is now nothing wanting, absolutely nothing but *faith,* to reunite the soul to God in perfect bridal beauty and joy.

Now remember, my dear brother, that faith, the very same faith, in principle, which is now required, was the bond of the soul's first union with God. What else could it be? *Distrust of God's love,* occasioned by the prohibition of the tree, broke the union. The tree, forbidden, represents the world. The soul, tried by the prohibition, fell into doubt about God's love, then it disobeyed—that broke the union, and since then it has sought its happiness in the world because it can look to no higher source for it.

Christ has brought back the soul to the very posture in which it stood before it fell. God loves you just as He then loved the soul, and has declared His love for you. You have only to believe it—you do believe it. What you are hoping and striving for, is a conscious love-relation between yourself and Christ, corresponding to the words—"My Beloved is mine, and I am His." You are convinced at last that this is the privilege of every soul—its normal condition—the best description of what all want, and of what it is the very design of the Gospel to give to all—every one of us, "whosoever will." Resting short of that, we are not really redeemed.

As to the way of attaining it, you are convinced further, that it is altogether of Grace—not at all of works. The great legal stumbling-block has been taken out of the way. It is not like the first trial, in which humanity stood for itself. Christ stands for you; and the faith which you already have, by which you are united to Him, makes your final triumph an absolute certainty.

But still there is a difficulty; you do not reach what your heart aspires to; you want special tokens of love—of His love—to confirm yours.

10

Your progress is very slow, and you cannot but attribute your failure to receive more of Him, to something yet lacking on your own part. You fear that faith does not comprehend all that is required, or if it does, that there is something yet wanting in yours. You see it must be generally true that faith is really the only "work" we can do, and the only condition which is required; but there is something about the manner in which faith affects our restoration which you may not yet quite understand. A great deal is said in the Gospel about "bearing the cross," etc., with our fidelity to which, our sanctification, or our enjoyment of the highest liberty of the soul, is intimately connected. According to Paul especially, the great assertor of "faith alone," the life-progress and perfection of the new man depends on the mortification of the old. Knowing this, you ask, What shall I do to hasten and perfect this work of mortification? What, for the entire destruction of the body of sin, or of my selfish and worldly desires? Anything for that deliverance by which my Beloved shall be mine—by which I shall know Him to be mine, and nothing remain to obstruct our communion, or my perfect knowledge of His will, and conformity to it, and my assurance that He is pleased with me. Does this depend on faith alone? Shall I reach it by still trusting entirely in Christ's justifying righteousness, and assuming that everything else will follow, putting all not only upon His love, but upon His faithfulness?

I assure you, my dear friend, there is no mistake about this matter at all. Sanctification (by which we mean entire devotion to God) is nothing else but the natural and necessary effect of a free justification—growing out of it just as the branches of a living vine grow out of their parent stock. But growth is, of course, a work of time; only hold on to the root. Let nothing interfere with the working of the doctrine of a free justification in the conscience—that is the root. According to the strength of the assurance which is thus imparted, your soul will gradually realize all your ideal of holiness. That is what unites you to Christ; there will be everything to try it, but trial will but strengthen the bond, while it destroys the root of selfishness.

And now, planting yourself on the Word of God that you are freely justified, saved, loved, your final triumph through Christ secure, are you not ready to wind the screw upon yourself a little tighter in the determination to hold on in prayer *until you get the blessing?* The blessing will be the consciousness that He is entirely yours. In reality He is so now, and you are never to doubt it. That doubt is the great temptation.

It is not an arbitrary appointment, but indispensable to our justification, and preparation for the glory that awaits us, that our faith should be tried. But a smile of Eternal Benignity has given you a distinct intimation, that after the endurance of a few farther trials, the effect of which, even while enduring them, will be to develop God and His love more and more in your consciousness, you shall reach the crown of all your aspirations.

V.

I THINK that we can say that our spiritual state is very much alike, allowing for the difference in outward circumstances: God not only our heart's desire but our soul's possession, so far at least as to make His holiness as dear as (I think dearer than) His goodness,—His moral beauty more attractive than benefits,—His trials almost as welcome as victories,—patience almost as natural (easy) as faith, because we so desire the purity in which they will terminate.

But while in one view I am as happy as I can hope to be here, in another I am greatly and constantly burdened. Why is God so little known, these perfections so little honored and esteemed, this moral beauty, shining as it does upon our apostate world through a medium (the Gospel) as free and large as the atmosphere, so little enjoyed? Not so much in contemplating the obstructions to the Gospel as in laboring to remove them do I find the work of my choice.

A man who has been delivered from oppression cannot much enjoy his freedom while his own flesh and blood are yet in bondage, unless he is making every effort for their deliverance. Oh, to make Christ transparent in everything, to be a living, speaking image of Him! * * * * * * * I cannot be at ease until I have started you in "Ecce Homo," the book of books among late publications. My enthusiasm for it arises partly from its superb workmanship, but much more from the new and strong humanitarian light which it throws upon the work of Christ, and from the perfect manner in which it meets what I now clearly see to be the great want of the time, a want from which we are all suffering—all who dare to think—though, until this remedy appeared, I, for one, scarcely allowed myself to see or feel it.

The book does not profess to give a complete view of the person and work of Christ. The sin which has alienated the soul from God, and the Redemption by which eternal life has been recovered, are barely acknowledged. The author gives us reason to believe that his views on these points will appear in another volume, which is in preparation. The present work is confined to a single line of thought, the object of which is to demonstrate the claims of Christ to the unbounded reverence of mankind, on grounds which every one, simply as having the common sympathies of men, is competent to appreciate, however ignorant of God.

For the want of some such representation more than from any other cause, as it seems to me, the intellect of this age is drifting away from Christianity. Certainly, the great miracle of Christianity is the character and life of its Founder, in connection with the beneficent change which they have given to the world's history. But these things have been studied so long and exclusively in connection with supernatural assumptions, and in the interest of purely theological theses, that they have lost their hold, or rather have never had any hold of the natural mind. That they may be seen by the common sense of mankind as a moral miracle of the highest order—seen in their absolute immeasurable superiority to all phenomena of the same kind which have occurred in the world, and felt as well as seen, they must be taken out of the domain of supernatural dogma and churchly tradition—out of the colored lights of scholasticism, and read simply as history, just as we read the history of any other great teacher, or world reformer.

This was just what was undertaken both by Strauss and Renan. They both represent the great intellectual want of the age in reference to Christianity—the want of an intelligible human or natural version of Christ's history and teachings, and of the relation of those teachings to the state of the world in His own time, and of human nature as it is always and everywhere, and how these alone account, without any supernatural assumptions, for its supremacy. Strauss failed, because the mythic view which he gives so violates men's faith in history, as to be more improbable than supernaturalism itself. Renan failed because his exposition of the history is a mutilation of its principal facts.

But what they failed to do this new genius has done marvelously. Take away from Christianity all that is supernatural, hush to silence all its dogmas, and it remains so superior to every effort of human wisdom that it must be seen to be Divine. All this in the hand of the author is as I suppose only a preparation to present the theology of Christianity in the same fresh, independent, incisive manner in his forthcoming work, as he has in this presented its morality. I should certainly find something to complain of in this volume, if it were not for the hope that the next may furnish the complement to many half or one-sided views which can hardly escape your notice. We shall do him injustice if passages in which he is merely limiting his utterance to the requirements of a particular class of men are considered as expressing his own entire belief.

The worst omen for the next volume is contained on the twelfth page of this—the reason for Christ being called the "Lamb of God," so different from that which the Baptist gives, viz., "He taketh away the sin of the world." There is nothing in the whole volume which really troubles me but that, and I wait impatiently to know if that interpretation is to give the key-note to his theology.

In looking back upon what I have written, I find I have been assuming that the author intended his book as an argument for the truth of Christianity. I am not sure that he had any such intention at all. However that may be, I have no doubt that his principal design is to divest the Christian system of the corruptions which have been attached (in his judgment) both to its morality and its spirituality, by the influence of ecclesiasticism and scholasticism. In this view you will derive your chief advantage from it. I shall send the book to you to-day.

In thinking of you this morning, I feel the most delightful certainty in regard to the end and design of God's dealings with you as well as with myself. "I will betroth thee unto Me for ever," expresses it all. Though, in order to know the grace of the Bridegroom we must be made to feel our unworthiness, and that our bliss in the end may be perfect we must be left sometimes desolate, yet one hour's vision of the Bridegroom—one moment's experience of His love, with the assurance that it shall never again be hidden, will abundantly recompense all our sorrows.

VI.

THE apostle prays for the Ephesians that they may comprehend what is the height, depth, etc.—the *fullness* of God's love—that they may know what is the hope of their calling, and what the riches of the glory of His inheritance in the saints, and what is the exceeding greatness of His power in them that believe. Thus he expresses the sum or end of all Christian attainments.

This is the end to which we are aspiring—after which we are reaching. The direct means of attaining this end is "the spirit of wisdom and revelation in the knowledge of Christ," which the apostle prays may be given to the Ephesian

Christians. As it is certain that God is more faithful in fulfilling His promises than we can be in pleading them, it may be asked, Why is not the condition here described realized at once in the experience of all Christians?

The main occasion of perplexity among Christians is, I apprehend, the same in all. "How is it possible that such as we should be the children of God and heirs of the promises?" Almost every one imagines some great defect in his Christian experience (inferring it from the deficiency in his life) which he fears may be fatal. Doubtless there are many who have reason for such fears, but they are not the persons who are commonly oppressed by them.

Let us consider then what is a proper foundation for confidence, or what should we answer if asked for the reason of the hope that is in us. When we think that the matter of our hope is nothing less than "an eternal weight of glory," a "kingdom prepared for us before the foundation of the world," how plain it is that no work of ours can be the foundation of such a hope, and how well is the real truth expressed by the phrase, "Christ in you the hope of glory." The incarnate God has purchased it for us by His own obedience unto death. Here is foundation enough surely. We can easily believe that He who gave His Son, His only Son, to die for us, will with Him also freely give us all things. But how do we know that He will give them to *us?* Because He has already given us "the earnest of His Spirit." How does this appear? In all the action of the new creature. What but the Spirit in us could give us such confidence toward God, conscious though we are of our fearful guilt and worthlessness, such joy and peace amidst the wreck of our earthly hopes, and, above all, such strength in the conflict of sin?

But, you may respond, this is just the point where my defect appears. It is just here that the promise seems to fail. A life-long struggle with sin I indeed endure, but why is it not more successful? The answer is, there is an order in the development of spiritual life as there is of natural life. You might as well ask why should we have to go through the dangers of infancy, and the trying experiences of a youthful course before we can reach the attainments of maturity, or why the seed should be so long buried in the earth before we see its result in a magnificent harvest. In answer to our first prayers we get the seed, and by "continuing in prayer," which is the chief exercise and expression of faith, and the spirit of which is kept up by opposing difficulties, the seed is gradually developed.

You say you do not want rapture—you want simply to live consistently. Are you perfectly sure that the consistency which you seek is not a meritorious personal distinction, and may you not be depending upon Grace as merely the *help* which is needful to attain it? Depend upon it, these incessant failures arise from erroneous views about the nature of sanctification—an error, however, which these failures are absolutely necessary to correct. Nothing but the very discipline which you are now enduring can teach you the truth. A little more patience, dear friend, and all will be clear. You will relinquish the pursuit of consistency and *cleave to Grace*, looking no farther. In proportion as you abide in Grace, you shall be consistent—and to abide in Grace you must abide in prayer.

I am becoming indifferent to everything else as a means of strength, or as a source of happiness, except simple prayer. I once cherished the hope of making such attainments as would raise me above the necessity of always confessing my wants and begging for help; but I find that constancy in prayer is the simple and sole condition of spiritual life. Many active duties must be performed, but prayer alone can teach us their nature and teach us to perform them aright. Christians are much hindered in growth by mistaking the regular performance of outward duties for inward prayer and perseverance—by depending on their duties instead of on the promises. Direct efforts to stir ourselves up to spiritual and holy exercises are seldom successful, I should say, when done with a view to meet the conditions of Divine promises. The spirit is obtained entirely by prayer in the name of Christ. He is granted wholly on account of Christ's oblation and intercession. Depending on the righteousness of Christ we cannot fail to receive the Spirit, and depending on the Spirit we cannot fail to be led into the path of duty.

Thus do you not see how abiding in Christ is necessary to our living in the Spirit, and how our not depending on the Spirit to lead us in the way of practical duty, involves as much unbelief as our not depending on the righteousness of Christ to secure our acceptance with God? It is as much the characteristic of a believer that he is led by the Spirit as that he trusts in Christ.

The power of Christians' prayers for each other has also become to me a matter of most earnest belief. And, in this connection, may I not request you to remember me in your prayers as much as you can. I am constrained, especially in my calling as a minister of Christ, to undertake duties for which in myself I am most unequal, and my conflict, I am well assured, shall have no end in this life. I am enjoying the strangest mercies, but these only increase my obligations. Need I describe to you the temptations and difficulties of the ministry? They may be given in a sentence,—an uncompromising adherence to the Word of God, an incessant conflict with the spirit of man. Public opinion is the Goliah which defies Israel, and if we would do anything for Israel's deliverance we must not shrink from this encounter. Our great danger is, that we shall be led almost unconsciously by public opinion and custom, in place of the Bible, and this will make us powerless indeed. Of all deficiencies of Christians, their praying so little or so faintly for ministers seems the strangest. If they had scriptural views of the nature of the work, they would pray for us without ceasing; and if they would only pray that we might be filled with such views ourselves, they would do immense service to the cause of Christ.

If I know myself, the one and only thing I want is to be stripped, entirely stripped of every form of pride—to die to myself, to live wholly upon the truth, faithfulness, and power of God. I have just one encouragement about myself, that is, that God knows my weakness, and I know His power.

VII.

YOU make rapid progress in evangelical ideas. I was particularly edified by what you said in your last letter upon the relations of the soul's exercises to Christ's righteousness, not as a means of safety, but of holiness. They express the very kernel of my present experience. I want holiness so much, that I might, perhaps, say I want nothing else. One additional grain of holiness, or conformity to God, with a consciousness that God was pleased with it, would outweigh a universe of any other kind of good; and how precious is the truth that Christ is *made* unto us sanctification as well as justification. * * * * * I agree with you entirely in what you say in regard to many of the books of modern type on the great subject of sanctification. I feel, as you do, a great lack, in some of them at least, of scriptural inspiration and confirmation of the views they express. It seems to me, for one thing, that without allowing much more for man's original natural similitude to God than they generally allow, no doctrine of sanctification, however scriptural and sacred it may appear, can be made distinct in theory, or efficient in practice.

My own hope, since the first moment of regenerate consciousness, has been founded in God the Father's love, of which the work of Christ has been not merely the expression but the *justification.* I mean the hope of my heart, for I confess that, for a long time, there was a variance between my religion and my philosophy. Owing to unfortunate teachings from books, and to other religious influences, I had received a system not only of doctrine but of experience, so unlike what I needed as to be a perfect incubus upon my nature. When I interpreted the Gospel according to my own instinctive sense of what I needed, I was obliged to believe that God stood to man in a relation of real Paternity, and that His love, free as the air I breathed, was the atmosphere in communication with which my life wholly depended: but, by my philosophy as then constructed, I had to regard man as merely one of God's works—a Thing. I could not understand, consistently with this philosophy, how God's love to man could be a real love founded on something in human nature which had an intrinsic value. According to this, I supposed that His love, as applied to the world, was merely a metaphor—meaning that His action toward the world, in the gift and sacrifice of Christ (the end of which was to accomplish some purpose of His own), was as *if* He loved it. This mechanical philosophy had so poisoned and stiffened my faith that it had nearly given up the ghost, and was almost entirely ineffective upon my moral and emotional nature. I could not conquer the world nor the fear of death, nor do anything, indeed, according to my ideal of Christian privilege and character. I suppose that, during all this time, there was a little fire, which accounts for the "smoking flax," but my life was felt to be one of miserable legal bondage. There was no lack of prayer and conscientious devotion to duty, with occasional flashes of hope that a better state was coming; yet the more I labored the more sensible I became of my bondage to sin, self, and the world, and, of course, the more unrelenting became the tyranny of the Law. And there I remained for a long time, like Samson in the Philistines' mill, though engaged in a never-ceasing struggle for freedom. Even when my acquaintance with the Gospel, interpreted as my own necessities would sometimes force me to interpret it, would occasionally let me out of prison for a brief time, it was rather as a reprieved criminal, subject to be remanded again by my short-comings, and very certain to be so remanded; for how to avoid these short-comings and their direful retribution, I knew not. I had continual desire and continual disappointment.

But after a long and dreary period there began to be, through various influences, a change produced in my philosophy, and thus a preparation for the recovery of my faith on rational grounds. I began now, from my intellect, to regard the soul not simply as *made* of God, but as *born* of Him—

not simply as the work of His hands, but as the offspring of His bosom—as something, therefore, which He could not but love, both for its intrinsic excellence and for His personal relation to it, which was as real as the parent to the child. I conceived now that God's love to man was one of which all earthly relationships were faint but genuine reflections. Thus I was brought back to a belief which, in the first instance, had been forced upon me by my desperate necessities, acted upon by the simple testimony of God to my heart in the Gospel revelation. Henceforth I had not a doubt that God loved sinful man, just as a father loves his prodigal son; that to reveal His love to him was the great object of the mission of Christ, and that faith in this love was the sole thing which made the Gospel the power of God unto salvation, from its first dawn in the trembling conscience, through all degrees of Christian experience, to its consummation in death and glory. How He who is so pure that the heavens are unclean in His sight *could* thus love sinful humanity, I know not, but both the fact and the method of it were settled in the infinite Sacrifice, that vicarious Sacrifice which is everything in Christianity, as sin is everything in humanity—its whole actual condition.

Protecting myself from the Divine holiness by the blood of the Lamb, I had no difficulty in acting on the general principle: "God so loved the world, that He gave His only begotten Son, that whosoever believeth on Him might not perish, but have everlasting life." I saw that whoever accepted Jesus Christ as the true manifestation of God, was, in Him, forever shielded from every principle but that of unobstructed love.

The sun had now risen, the shadows had begun to disperse. The love of God, long the object of my soul's faith, had become also the cardinal hinge of my philosophy. In various and subtle ways these new views gave a new spring to my spiritual powers. There was a meaning to my desires for holiness, and a life to my prayers for it which were quite new and glorious. I felt that I had nothing to do for justification, and for purification, but to be forever receiving Christ's love and salvation, and that coming to Christ is the effect of the Father's drawing. I saw God, in Christ, reconciling the world unto Himself, and a vital faith in this truth secured the thing I had always been seeking for—deliverance from bondage, legal and worldly.

Since that time, for long, long years, the trials of life, to which there is no cessation, have been sustained by a succession of most living experiences and manifestations of God's goodness—by revelations of God's love in Christ, coming almost as often as I have felt any occasion for them—always when trial has been unusual—until at length the promise is almost literally fulfilled, "Your peace shall be like a river." Any doubts which I may have about my state are so transient and superficial as to be scarcely worth considering. And the same thing may be said about worldly trials, whether of success or disappointment. Death is no longer an object of dread, and as to the final judgment, my *principles* will not allow any concern about that; for the basis of all my enjoyment and hopes is the assurance that I can never come into condemnation.

And yet this long seeking of deliverance in a legal way was of use to me. Its effect was to produce a thorough consciousness of corruption, and thus to make me understand practically the full significance of God's love, especially as expressed through justification by Grace, through faith alone. My relaxed hold of this doctrine was the real cause of my troubles. I supposed, and had no doubt, from the earliest bad symptoms, that all my difficulties arose from the want of sanctification; and hence how to attain it was the only question which seemed to have any significance. I naturally wanted freedom from bondage, and, *therefore*, I wanted sanctification, supposing always that to be its essential condition or cause, whereas it really is its effect. An eternal obstacle prevented the attainment of freedom or holiness on that principle, for it was only a refined method of seeking justification by Law. Our union to God, the soul of which is desire to serve Him, must be the fruit of that life which comes only from our belief in the unchanging favor of God to us, for Christ's sake. Then sanctification follows of course—a principle of love which makes you work for God just as heartily (but without the least care) as you once labored for yourself.

How happy I am in the certainty, my dear brother, that for you, as well as for myself, everything in God's dealings with us will but swell the manifestation of His love in the end. * * * *

I should be ashamed to have written so much about myself if I had not been writing as brother to brother—as friend to friend; and if I did not hope that what I have said might tend to strengthen you. My prayer when I first knew you was, "O that I might not die until I have been enabled to show him the way to the heart of God!"

VIII.

MY special reason for sending you Olshausen at this time is the strong impression I have that the most important thing in order to your peace and progress is, that the power of religious emotion which in you is very strong, and yet not too strong, should be balanced by a corresponding depth of religious knowledge. The whole Christian world, I believe, are united in pronouncing Olshausen's as one of the best, if not the very best, commentary on the New Testament, as a whole, which we have.

Let me say, however, that I have no faith in your getting any good from him except by making him a long study. It will greatly tax your attention for a while, and may even perplex you;

but after you have read and pondered a great deal, you will find yourself beginning to get a profounder insight into the New Testament, and into spiritual mysteries, than you ever had before. It was by reading Olshausen on the Romans, that I first came to a clear, perfect, loving faith in the atonement, in which I have been growing ever since.

With wonder and joy, my dear brother, have I been reading the book you sent to me, Faber's "Creator and Creature." Did ever a book more completely fulfill the promise of its title, "The Wonders of Divine Love?" Some other books have given us these wonders in rills and streamlets; here is an attempt, and as successful as words can make it, to describe the Ocean. And yet the book has raised a conflict in my mind between commendation and criticism—commendation of the artist and criticism of the theologian. Fascinated by the beauty and fervor of the artist, and finding also so much that was divinely true, as well as humanly beautiful, in his production, I deliberately determined, in my first reading, to repress the spirit of theological criticism—to believe it true while I was reading it, and if there was a mistake to correct it afterwards.

I must say, looking at Faber's system in the light of a cooler judgment, it seems to me that its power lies in its being a system of Christian casuistry in which the heart must be the chief dictator. In other words, as a system of theology in which the understanding must be chief dictator, Faber's philosophy is a failure. As a view of the Divine relations to the universe, and as a solution of cosmical problems, it cannot be accepted.

Edwards, on "God's Chief End in Creation," bears the same relation to Faber's "Creator and Creature," that Newton's "Principia," the design of which was to demonstrate the principles or laws of the natural universe, does to some eloquent modern exposition of their uses. Amazingly interesting and beautiful, and helpful to the needs of my heart, as Faber's application of the doctrine of God's love is, I must say, I greatly feel the need also of the other element which Edwards' treatise furnishes. The difference is, that the one absolutely satisfies the understanding of the truth of a principle which had already possessed the heart—the other only intensifies the emotions which grow out of faith in the principle.

Neither am I sure whether Faber's views of the Divine goodness can be entirely harmonized with our necessary conceptions of the Divine holiness. The ruling impression made upon my mind by reading the book was, that in God's relations to man, we are to conceive of holiness as subordinate to goodness; and yet I may be wrong in my impressions and judgment of its principles and assertions.

In the treatment of perfectly holy beings, Divine love cannot be overstrained,—holiness and love, even love to individuals, are convertible terms. But in the education of such a being as man, even regenerate man, though the expression of Divine goodness cannot be too large, provided it be proportionate to the expression of holiness, the want of the due representation of the latter detracts just so much from the power of the other. The general objection that I have to Faber's view (as I understand it) of God's relation to man, is not by any means that it makes God's love to man too generous, which is impossible—but that he does this in such a way that there is danger it will tend to diminish my respect for the Creator—or, which is the same thing, my estimate of the nature and desert of sin, and consequently of the grace, the real grace, which appears in the Atonement.

Take, for example, the brilliant idea with which the book opens, which so fascinated you, as by its plausibility and ingenuity it did me; the idea that *love to the future man* was the ruling motive of the eternal counsels,—sin itself, with the atonement made for it, being but parts of a plan, the sole object of which was to give that love an extraordinary field for development. I must say that while such an idea fills me at first with rapture unspeakable, considered as an illustration of the power of Divine benignity and condescension, I find in a little while that it has dimmed the luster of the Divine holiness. I have lost a portion of my respect for God, through the conception which at first seemed omnipotent in securing my love to Him. Grateful as such a view is to my natural feelings, I cannot bring it into any harmony with my reason, and it does a still worse violence to my spiritual affections.

Above all other things I want a God whom I can *honor*—honor for His greatness, for His purity, for His immutability, for the qualities, in a word, which command *His own self-respect*. If, in addition to these, I find that He is capable also of the tenderest affection for such a creature as I am, then indeed my bliss is complete. But to have Him make me, or the like of me, the end of creation, I cannot believe it, and if I could, it would not give me the highest joy of which I am consciously capable. But beside the irrationality of such a theory, its inharmoniousness with our deepest spiritual intuitions, there is an invincible difficulty in reconciling it at all with the history of the race.

But I can go no farther—though I want very much to show you how such a man could fall into such a theory. It belongs to the genius of the Roman Catholic Church, the whole aim of which is not to present the truth as it is objectively, but to devise every manner of subjective exhibition by which it can win human nature to its embrace. It was just this which gave rise to the reaction of Protestantism, which is an endeavor to bring these thousand Roman Catholic inventions to the simple standard of reason and the Scriptures, in doing which we have undoubtedly gone too far the other way,—in our zeal to preserve the rational and Divine element, taking too little pains to associate with it the emotional and human.

How wonderfully beautiful were the two poetical gems of Faber you so kindly transcribed for me —the very richest of the kind I ever read, and altogether unique. Have you ever known a richer nature than that man's? I have also read his "Spiritual Conferences," and his "Growth in Holiness," which, notwithstanding serious defects in the latter, have increased my admiration for the variety of his gifts. Half of his power lies in his wonderful talent for expression, though the other half, arising from the purity and fervor of his thoughts, would distinguish him sufficiently.

I am going on famously with my studies, and in perfect health, but with such a sense of sin, not my own merely, but the sin and corruption of humanity, as would make life a terrible burden but for the constantly developing revelation of God's character and purposes. "Art Thou not from everlasting, O Lord my God,—we shall not die."

IX.

WHILE nothing would give me such pleasure as to spend the whole day in narrating the progress of the "Holy War" in the hidden man of the heart, I must send you a dispatch in a few sentences, like Lord Raglan's from the field of conflict,—I wish I could say like Napoleon's in one respect,—or like Com. Perry's, "We have seen the enemy and they are ours!" To see the enemy, by the way, is the hardest part of it. What hours I have spent turning my spiritual telescope in all directions, to get a just idea of his strength and his movement. As to *God's love to me*, dear friend, your solicitude that I should be duly impressed with it may be dismissed. That is the one thing that is clear. It is a fire within me which I trust no waters can ever drown. More than this, I *see the end.* It cannot fail. I am not fighting uncertainly; and yet, with every advantage, it is a most protracted business. "Ye have need of patience." The theory, or "plan of the war," is perfectly plain. The great point is to get the will perfectly free—detached from every terrene sticking-place, so that it will answer to the slightest motion of the

Divine Spirit, and then, as the Divine Spirit vitalizes it, to press onward and still onward, watching always against the new and increasingly subtle manœuvres of the enemy, until he is worn out, and the communion of our spirit with the Divine becomes perfectly *simple.* How nearly I shall reach this point while in the enemy's country, God only knows; but my course is plain. Christ has made me free if I will but use my freedom.

"Man," says Vinèt, "in respect of good or of God, is a living channel, personal and free. God is the Fountain which flows through the channel." "All strength in religion, all efficiency," says Manning, "is but the effect of the inexhaustible fullness of the Spirit flowing through a will holy and free, and filling the whole spirit and soul of man." To reach this freedom, then, by faith and self-mortification, the result of faith, is all our work. The enemy is strongly intrenched, and makes havoc sometimes by his sorties, but we are no longer the besieged, but the besiegers. Our lines are narrowing every day, and, more than that, our Prince is on the way. He will not tarry—the first glimpse of Him will make our enemy an easy prey—then we shall be free indeed and free forever.

You kindly ask God that the residue of my years may be years of peace. "The peace of God which keepeth the heart and the mind;" freedom from an evil conscience—that indeed is indispensable; the want of that, in constancy and patience, was my misery for years. I trust, indeed, that I shall never know that misery again. But no other peace do I desire but that which is gained by a conquest which I am sure cannot be fully gained while in this tabernacle. The one earthly attainment which I do want, is such power over myself as shall make me entirely free to labor directly and intensely for others; not publicly or by preaching merely, or at all even, if I can do as much by prayer or private methods.

You tell me you cannot balance your account with me in correspondence. I feel the reverse to be the truth. Every letter which I have ever received from you has given me a heavenward impulse; and if they had contained nothing but the assurance of your concern and prayer for my spiritual welfare, giving me an example of a man who can pray so earnestly for another, to say nothing of that other being myself, I should feel them to be among my richest treasures. * * * * * *

I have labored too much in my life to cultivate certain subjective frames—which at best are but a sieve that lets out the living water as fast as it flows in, or a stream which in a little while dries up. But I do feel at last, that the only way of living is to *keep close to the Fountain;* to trust God's words, whatever may be your frames,—His love to you, not yours to Him. He will do everything for you; not the very thing you ask, perhaps, in all cases, though sometimes even that; and if not that, something far better.

I could tell you some strange things which have happened to me of late, showing how *low* He will descend to meet a real exigency of one of his weakest ones. How visible His Providence sometimes is! If we would only trust Him fully, our whole life would be a record of strength ordained out of weakness.

Dear friend, I know your heart—you want above all things that Christ should be glorified in you. But trial develops a thousand other wants which stand in the way of the realization of the great one; these will become less and less. It takes time to get them out of the way. Your mind is now on the right track, most certainly. What you want, is not the knowledge of redemption, but a personal union with the Redeemer; not a seeking to comprehend, but to be apprehended by Him.

* * * * * My work, suspended for some time, is renewed with the ardor of high expectation. I have moments of such assurance—days and weeks I should rather say—after a conflict with some great doubt or sin, when it seems to me if it were God's will I could not but be most sweetly resigned to death. No words can express my conviction of the emptiness of earthly joys, even of the dearest of them, in comparison with growth in holiness, or that moral state in which Divine enjoyment is the rule, and not the exception. That explains my willingness to die. What is it to die, but to be entirely holy and perfectly blest?

Dear brother, how my heart throbs for you. May God give you a hundred-fold more (and I know He will) than you can ask or think. If I can feel such a longing for your spiritual emancipation, what must Christ feel? My own feelings furnish the best comment on his words, "Neither shall any pluck them out of my hands." This is our security.

X.

NOTHING but the hope of more time (always a bad calculation) has moved me to postpone my answer to your letter. You wish me to give you some of my ideas as to the nature of prayer; and it is a subject upon which I have been thinking with much more than usual interest of late.

Have you ever thought much on the relations of prayer to the unregenerate? In one sense the Lord is, indeed, the Saviour of all men. He is their natural Preserver. As such, He is good to all, and His tender mercies are over all His works. Whether we are His people or not, and whether we pray to Him or not, He forgiveth all our iniquities—that is, He suspends His judgments; He healeth all our diseases; He crowneth our lives with loving-kindness and tender mercies. But it is common for people to look upon these blessings as the fruit of their prayers, and to regard them as proofs of a special interest in the favor of God—a most ungenerous sentiment in its bearings upon the character of the Deity, and most destructive in its final action upon the interests of those who indulge it.

It is natural for men in any distress, whether of body or soul, to cry to their Maker—a circumstance which, in a vast majority of cases, merely proves the intensity of their distress—not a prayerful mind. And the fact that they commonly find relief, whether of conscience or body, instead of being a proof that God has been moved by their prayers, is just a proof, on the other hand, that God is good even to the prayerless. God relieves them, not on account of their prayers, but for the purpose of leading them to prayer; not because they are penitent, but to lead them to repentence; not because they are His people, but that they may be induced to give up their sins and to become His people.

But the prayers of the regenerate go up from the depths of spiritual tribulation. The decisive question is, Do we continue to pray, like the poor publican—have we not exalted ourselves, or been exalted, by the perversion of Divine favors, to an esteem of ourselves somewhat greater than we felt when we first beat upon our breasts, and cried for mercy? Do we still continue that cry, amidst all our temptations to pride, selfish ease, ungodliness, unrighteousness?

"Say what is prayer, where it is prayer indeed?
The mighty utterance of a mighty need.
That man is praying, who doth press with might,
Out of his darkness into Heaven's own light."

Prayer is the *cry* of the people of God—a cry which is wrung from them by their grievances. This idea is brought out largely by the Apostle in the eighth of Romans, where, after describing the travail of the whole creation by reason of sin, he adds; "And not only they, but ourselves also, which have the first-fruits of the Spirit, even we ourselves groan within ourselves," etc. The "poor widow," also (Luke xviii., 2–4), represents God's people individually and in the aggregate; the necessities of the regenerate—"Avenge me of my adversary;" the perplexities of the regenerate—"He would not for a while;" the ground of their confidence for deliverance at last—"Shall not God avenge His own elect, who cry day and night unto Him?"

According to the Scriptures, according to all experience, prayer, reduced to its essence, is simply this—the groaning of a soul in bondage, its breathing and panting after spiritual liberty. This only is prayer; and the people who thus pray are God's elect, and He will speedily avenge them.

Though, like little children, they only *feel* their grievances, without being able to tell what they are, that is the very thing—" They know not what to ask for as they ought." Therefore, God has but little regard to their words. It is their groans that He listens to—the pantings and breathings of His spirit within them for things which cannot be uttered, which cannot be asked for—only in general. They want liberty—liberty from sin, from the devil and his temptations, enlargement in the enjoyment and service of God; but how they shall attain this, or what it depends on, that is beyond their understanding. The system of relations by which they are surrounded is a mixed system, composed both of good and evil, but they cannot make the discrimination. Therefore their appeal is to God—they cry to Him day and night. Borne down by a growing accumulation of evils, they sink and sink till they fall back at last upon the Everlasting Arm—that Arm which from the first was laid underneath them, but now they *feel* it, and, therefore, more and more earnestly they supplicate its direct interposition. They no longer depend upon themselves at all. They rest upon the Rock of Ages. God knows everything; God can *do* everything, God is love; He is their light, He also will become their salvation.

But you will ask, what is the place of faith in prayer, and what the ground of it, of which I have as yet said little. Our Saviour does not say of the publican, that he *dared not* so much as lift his eyes to Heaven, though that is a common interpolation —as though it were essential to humble prayer that the soul should not expect, or at least should be very doubtful of obtaining the blessing which it asks for. Is not this the idea which many associate with the prayer of the publican? and nothing shows in a stronger light how little the subject of prayer, and especially of humble prayer, is understood.

If there is any one principle which is peculiarly scriptural, it certainly is this—that in making our requests known unto God, there is just as much humble prayer as there is of real confidence. "Spiritual agony in prayer," is a phrase that may be much misunderstood and perverted. Some receive from it only the idea of a person laboring under a deep conviction of one's ruin, connected with a vehement desire for deliverance, and a determined resolution to obtain it, and it certainly does convey this idea; but if that were all, the agony, however great, would be very useless—indeed, it is the very evil from which we have everything to fear. The sinking fears, and the flickering hopes are the evils with which we have to contend, and there is but one principle upon which we can do it—that which lays hold upon the blessing, and makes it ours. This is faith, "the substance of things hoped for, the evidence of things not seen." This is the principle especially which agonizes or wrestles—not in the way of vehement cryings, nor in the way of long confessions, necessarily, but in the way of importunately watching for, and faithfully expecting, the hand of the Most High. "My soul," says the Psalmist "waiteth for the Lord, more than they that watch for the morning." This is the principle which will lead the soul simply to wrestle, and neither sleep nor move till the day dawn, and the Day Star arise. This is faith. Towards our actual redemption we do absolutely nothing—no more than a man does toward making the sun shine. *Will we wait till it comes?* That is the agony.

Our whole danger arises from two kinds of temptation. On the one hand, the invincibleness of our sins fills us with despair. Our strength has often been tried by them before, and though there has been no lack of prayer, resolution, or any of the common means, yet how often have our enemies overcome us. Should we listen then, only to the dictates of experience, we might decide at once that our case was hopeless without a struggle. That is our first temptation.

But it may work the other way; that is, instead of concluding from our past reverses that we had better do nothing, but yield at once, we conclude on the other hand that we will now do more than we ever did before; we will now make our final and decisive effort. As we are thus disentangled from one temptation, we are immediately liable to another—that of moving in our own strength at the first beck of hope, upon the first appearance of light, whether it be the light of a meteor which shoots athwart the gloom, or of the Sun of Righteousness, with healing in his beams.

These are the dangers, from which we can only be delivered by the prayer of faith. What is the ground of this faith? It is the Gospel. "With the Lord there is mercy, and with Him is plenteous redemption." What is mercy? favor to the unworthy—that is to *me*. What is redemption? deliverance for the captive, that is for *me;* and this is "with the Lord," who knows how to apply it, and when to apply it, infinitely better than any creature can prescribe. This is the ground of our confidence—that there is salvation in the Lord, and just such a salvation as we need—pardon for the guilty, redemption for the enslaved, *purchased* for us by the precious blood of the Redeemer, through whose merits we may "come *boldly* unto the throne of grace, that we may obtain mercy, and grace to help in time of need."

This is the ground upon which we wrestle—with unbelief, on the one hand, which tells us that our hope shall never be realized, and with pride on the other, which tells us it is already fulfilled. "Blessed are those servants whom their Lord, when He cometh, shall find *watching*. I tell you He will gird Himself and serve them." The principal source of our difficulties in prayer is the subtlety of Satan, the end of all his devices being to make us distrust God. Though prayer is the vital necessity of the Christian, there is, in almost all cases, something in the aspects of Providence, inward or outward, or both (in the condition of the atmosphere), which makes prayer (breathing) without intermission a great trial. The tendency is to faint. This is the condition, more or less, of all prayer in the present life. While our necessities compel us to pray, other conditions present a constant temptation to discouragement.

Now my true yoke-fellow, my brother beloved, I want to encourage you. You know what a "poor widow" I have been. I never really thought the Judge unjust, but little did I suppose He would become *my avenger*. I feel it now in the lowest depths of my nature—not for *my* crying, but for the crying of my Head, my Saviour, with whom I am one. Only in so far as we have an identity of interest with Him, or in so far as the language of our deepest heart is, "Thy will, not mine, be done," can we offer believing prayer.

This a long letter, and yet there are other aspects of this subject—its relations especially to our temporal wants, to our prayers for others, etc.,—which I would like to consider. But the principle is the same—it must be *believing prayer* in all cases. This is the key which opens Heaven. May God teach us how to turn it.

XI.

MY letters have happened to come to you very much in a cluster. I trust it may be a cluster from the brook Eshcol (see Numbers xiii. 23), designed to help your unbelief as well as to strengthen the Joshua who, by God's command, is leading you into the Land of Promise.

I want to cheer you by telling you that the Lord is with me as almost never before since the beginning of my war against "the darkness of this world;" and how much of my comfort arises from knowing that I can conquer for others as well as for myself. I have long enjoyed all that kind of inward peace which the testimonies in the Scriptures respecting God's forgiving mercy and the efficacy of Christ's atoning death, are adapted to give the agitated conscience, and for years I have been accustomed to rest all my hopes upon them—a hope which has prompted me to a life of prayer, and to a sincere and cordial endeavor for the most inward conformity to the Divine will. As far as I know myself, my trust in and attachment to the doctrines of Grace have arisen quite as much from their tendency to purify as to pacify. But I have wanted more than this; and God has been pleased most graciously to grant it in a *view of Himself*, which I have had for a short time past, which has been entirely irrespective of any assumed personal relations to Him. There have been moments in which I have had a sense of the glory of God, not, as some have said, as much as I could bear in the body, but rather the lowest degree, probably, in which such a bliss is ever imparted—enough, however, to give me a very clear idea of the nature of Heaven, or of the manner in which, immediately after death, the soul is perfected. In these moments self-regard, which in its supremacy I am sure is the whole sin of my nature, is a feeling of which I have been scarcely conscious. I want no other Heaven than that which the continuance of such a sense of the Divine glory would give me; though I cannot doubt that, in order to our complete felicity, other elements will be added to this, such as communion with holy beings, and especially as I now strongly believe, with those whom we have loved on earth.

That is, indeed, a wonderful joy which springs from a sense of God's personal love to us,—to declare which to us, and reveal it in us, Christ tells us in the last verse of His Intercessory prayer, was the end of all His work here upon earth. "That the love wherewith Thou hast loved me" (think of that—the very love with which He loved Christ) "may be in them, and I in them," the last clause being explanatory of the other; for it is just in so far as Christ dwells in our hearts by faith, that we are "rooted and grounded" in the assurance of God's love to us, and able to comprehend its fullness. (See Ephesians iii., 14–20.)

But we must not suppose that the joy here promised arises only from knowing that God loves us in particular. That would be but a poor conception of the "riches of God's inheritance in the saints"—a rich joy indeed considered as an equivalent for our sufferings, but O, how mean when measured by the soul's capacity, and how much more so when considered as the measure of Christ's reward—the reward of His sufferings. We are capable of an infinitely higher joy than that which springs from a sense of personal safety or personal distinction. Was that, do you think, Christ's joy, of which we are told that we shall be partakers, His own personal glory, simply? The manifestation of the Father's glory, the glory of God, that was the end of Christ's sufferings, and the "joy that was set before Him," which enabled Him to endure them. And so the vision of God's glory, which, in its bearings on our own destiny, and that of our race, is nothing else but the *vision of His love*—that is what the soul is made for—that is the measure of its capacity; and as this is revealed to us which it can only be by being revealed in us, it becomes a source of joy unmeasurable.

As light alone is the source of all sentient enjoyment, as without it all the other adaptations of nature so infinite and varied for the happiness of sentient beings would but intensify their misery, making their capacity for happiness but a capacity for pain, so "the light of the knowledge of the glory of God in the face of Jesus Christ," revealed partially here and perfectly hereafter, is the fountain of spiritual and eternal joy. This is the joy which Christ has promised us; the joy of *knowing* that *God is love;* the joy of drinking forever from the living and exhaustless fountain of God's eternal perfection—from the "rivers of His pleasure."

But this glory to be a source of living joy must be revealed *in* us,—see Romans viii. 18,—and in our present state this can only be done through suffering. Our first joy arises from a sense of God's kindness to us personally—in forgiving our iniquities, and healing our diseases, in hearing our prayers, scattering our darkness, and strengthening us in the hour of our need ; and pretty much all of our joy in this world has this particular character. In order to raise us, God first condescends to us, to our lowest conditions. When "the days of our mourning shall be ended," God will be "our everlasting light," a light never intermitted. Here, beside being so limited in measure, it is also ever alternating with darkness. Joy grows out of sorrow. Only through personal suffering from a sense of sin, and personal deliverance, the result of strong crying and tears, is this glory revealed in us, and then but partially though sufficiently for our progress. The promise of Christ is not that we shall never have sorrow, or that a time will come to us in this life when we shall not have it any more; for the present is intended to be a state of temptation, and, therefore of affliction; but that our sorrow shall be ever turning into joy, until at last it shall be swallowed up in joy eternal and unchanging.

Hold fast, then, my dear fellow-soldier of Christ, that liberty from legal bondage with which He has made you free. On your success in grasping and maintaining this principle of freedom, or confidence in the word and work of Christ alone, depends the brightness of your future. All your failures will arise from faltering here. Get round this one point, and *keep getting round it*, for this will still be the main labor, and all your way (though you see it not to be so, but think it otherwise, perhaps,) will be a march to glory.

In a little while, a very little while (I see it as distinctly as if it were right before me), you will feel an angel touching you. "O, child, greatly beloved," will be his language, "you have won the crown!" A vision of the glory to be revealed will put to rout your temptations. Of the power of these temptations I am well aware; and if I am so, and think of you constantly with such a power of sympathy, how much more the Captain of your salvation—He who was made perfect through suffering, that is, perfect as a *Leader*. Think you that He will always leave you in your present perils? No; the world is not going to conquer you. Your prayer was heard from the beginning.

Pray on; pray ever. The crown of purity above, and the assurance of it here—a token of the love of Jesus, in comparison with which what is everything but ashes,—will soon be yours.

Of one thing be ever assured; that while he has breath to pray, even while the lamp is flickering in its socket, and in worlds beyond, if that be possible, your cause shall be the cause of your friend.

XII.

I HAVE been looking lately into several books of the day which record the experience of a great and happy change which occurs often to those who have long been Christians—sometimes called Sanctification, or Perfection, or the Higher Life, or Assurance, or Second Conversion. I find a great difference in these books, some of them being worth little or nothing, and none of them proving (and very few of them attempting or claiming to prove) the doctrine of entire perfection in this life. Some of them are most delightful, and I feel that whoever would criticise them should read them many times upon his knees.

Where there is a fabric of precious truth, based it may be, in part at least, on a foundation of errors, to decompose such a structure so as clearly to distinguish the human from the Divine—the precious and the enduring from the perishable—is a work of no ordinary responsibility. One hardly dares to allow a critical spirit even ordinary sway, lest the heart may suffer by the loss of some portion of what is valuable.

Yet I think we ought to be on our guard against being unduly influenced by those books, where the writers in laying out all their power in explaining the immediate and secondary agencies upon which the spiritual life depends—the agencies of the human will—unintentionally, to be sure, but often too effectually impair the symmetry of the great scheme of Grace. I have often felt in reading these books how desirable it was to connect more closely with such views of creature agency, and the necessity of holiness, the doctrines of total natural depravity, of regeneration wholly by the Spirit (not by truth, but by power), and of justification, entire and unchangeable, by faith in its simplest form.

My own spiritual necessities demand on the one

hand holiness, as I want life; and on the other hand I feel an equal necessity for the Pauline principles respecting sin, justification, and redemption—*purchased* redemption. It seems to me that many, if not most, of the errors in the views of some of the modern writers upon this great subject of sanctification arise from an attempt to graft the peculiar truths of Revelation on certain principles of natural reason—to bridge the gulf which separates nature from Grace. They virtually substitute a personal for an imputed righteousness as the basis of our communion with God. Their views of Christian character, or what it should be, are excellent; but when they speak of this as a perfect state, or make it a ground of acceptance with God, they virtually overthrow the Gospel. They exhibit truly and beautifully the nature of holiness—the feelings of the regenerate soul towards God—what faith is, of its basis in our nature, and of its relations to all the other acts and duties of the Christian life; but they often fail sadly in describing the *way* of life—the way in which we become children of God—the way in which faith is produced.

In my earnest desire to absorb all that is good from such books, I have frequently wondered why it was that while my spiritual pulsations were much accelerated, there seemed to be little gain of real nourishment for the soul; or what the influence was which could so powerfully affect the branches of my spiritual being, beautifying and even quickening them for a while, while it did nothing to invigorate, but to speak plainly, rather tended to weaken the root.

I think it must be that the celebrated William Law belonged to this class of authors, of whom Mr. Wesley attests, that while his writings greatly excited him to vigilance and effort, they at the same time prevented him from duly appreciating the most cardinal and life-giving truth of the Gospel.

To those who are immovably settled in the fundamental position of justification by righteousness imputed, and are at the same time earnestly pursuing the righteousness inherent, no harm may come; but upon many of the weak and unstable there is danger that the general effect of such works will be to depreciate still farther in their estimation the grand doctrine of the Gospel, and lead them to substitute a subtle species of self-righteousness for the "Righteousness of God."

I find that the moment I lose sight of the distinction between the general principles of my faith, in which I have once been settled, and the particular improvements which come by experience and reflection, attaching to the latter the same importance which I give to the former, I am in danger of studying only the barrenness of my soul. Indeed, I am entirely opposed to all theories of sanctification which tempt us to rest our confidence in subjective changes. Aside from their being so unscriptural, they lead us to make some emotional experience our goal, a sure way generally of missing it, or if successful, of being misled by it afterwards.

I need not tell you that I object also to all theories of instantaneous sanctification as being not only unscriptural, but contrary to the deep and almost universal experience of the Christian life. I should not dispute the attainableness of entire sanctification in this life, in the sense of its being merely a higher degree of the spirit into which every child of God is born, and which is just as entire, in the proper or strict sense of the word, in the babe as in the man.

My heart certainly inclines me strongly to the belief of a state attainable in this life as different from the one commonly rested in as it is from absolute perfection. I believe that there is such a thing as perfect peace, and as abiding as it is perfect. "The God of all grace, who hath called you to His eternal glory by Jesus Christ, after that ye have *suffered* for a while, make you perfect, stablish, strengthen, settle you." What does that mean? Our sufferings arise from the power of our earthly affections which are not in harmony with God's law. These separate us from God, obstruct our progress in the spiritual life, and cause darkness, perplexity, and mourning. They specially hinder our faith. The promise is, that after we have suffered from these causes for a while, long enough to give us an humbling acquaintance with ourselves, and to make us duly appreciate the grace of God, He will by His Spirit abate their force. He will so break their power that they shall no more interrupt our peace and our communion with Him as they once did. As for a little while (comparatively) the strength of sin, or at least our difficulties with it, seemed rather to increase, so after a while grace shall increase, sin shall die sensibly from day to day, and the hope of deliverance shall be so strong, faith shall be so energetic, as gradually to raise us above our temptations.

The truth is, there are two kinds of perfectionists—those who really want *holiness*, and those who only want *rest*. The latter, tired of incessant conflict, get rest from it by assuming that the law does not require quite as much as they had been taught to believe, and that perfection consists in doing the best they can. The other class, not so much tired of conflict as sick of sin, without changing their theoretic views, only make a more thorough application of them to their own individual conditions. They spare not the right hand, nor the right eye. They are determined to enter into Life. Allured by the wonderful love of God in justifying them freely—in absolving them from all condemnation, though at the expense of a Saviour's blood, ashamed of receiving so much and returning so little, inflamed with hatred to sin not so much on account of the pain which it gives to themselves (viewed in a selfish way), as on account of the dishonor which it does to God and their Saviour, they are thus prepared to see far more in the promises of freedom than they ever cared to see before—in short, the love of sin having received a mortal blow from what is called a sight of the Cross, or, expressed more practically, from a thorough conviction of the *design* of Christ's death, they are determined that sin shall not live in them. This leads them to discover its existence in secret, subtle, but most powerful forms, which perhaps they had never suspected, to which at any rate they had been so vitally attached, that to part with them was like parting with life. Upon the surrender of these, they find the sanctifying process becomes a matter of such sensible consciousness, that if the intellect is not as clear and discriminating as the heart is warm, they will be likely to consider it their first experience of holiness; or, if they are very uninformed by previous reflection in the system of the Bible—if all their knowledge of it has been by tradition—in their first attempts at theorizing for themselves, they may adopt for a little while the fancy of perfection, from which, however, their experience will soon dislodge them.

Of all delicate and difficult things, the most difficult is to describe to another in such a manner that he will be really helped by it, the process of dying to self and the law through faith in Christ. Of one thing I am sure; I find that just in so far as I yield to the Gospel persuasion, in spite of every inward suggestion to the contrary, that on God's part all is love, free and unconditional, my selfish bonds are broken, my response to that love becomes more distinct and certain, and whatever there is of self-life remaining (and who can describe its tenacity), whatever of undue worldly affection, or of duty withheld, my jealousy, like a powerful flame, searches it out and consumes it. I have learned at length that seeking to know how far purity may be attained, is the same as asking to what extent may we get rid of self-righteousness—for the two are exactly parallel. The more we get rid of self-dependence, and really depend upon Christ, the more purity shall we attain. When the idol of self-righteousness has been utterly demolished, when we have nothing left in ourselves to live upon, and live wholly upon the grace of God in Christ, we then shall have real purity of heart—so perfectly adapted is the Gospel method (which in theory seems to befriend sin), when thoroughly applied, to utterly exterminate it.

For myself, I am entirely satisfied with the way in which God is leading me. I feel the burden of sin heavily, and no dependence upon my own efforts to lighten it. But I am growingly submissive to God's way of deliverance, and humbly confident of complete redemption in due season. I have a much stronger reliance than I formerly had on Christ—that though He may not give me a thorough victory in this life—though my trial may be more protracted than when I had a stronger self-reliance I thought it would be, He will never leave me to the dominion of sin, and will fully satiate my spiritual desires at last.

XIII.

I WANT very much to talk with you about an expression of yours, in our last conversation. "I have no hope of obtaining the blessing in this life, though I am sure of its reality," and more to the same effect. Now, let me say, that you *may* expect "the blessing"—if by it you mean, as I suppose you do, decided progress in the Christian life, and an assurance that your final victory is certain. I once had grave doubts of this myself—that is, whether sanctification on earth amounted to anything, or whether there was any certain progress in the Christian life. What I saw in so many, and what I felt in myself, made me very heart-sick and discouraged. "Wilt Thou be altogether unto me as waters that fail?" But God has long since vindicated both His goodness and His wisdom in my spiritual allotments. By the very methods which I thought were going to ruin my hopes, He has saved them. I believe if He had given me my desires for what I prayed for as spiritual freedom, I could not have attained to the knowledge that I now have of sin and grace; and imperfect as my holiness still is, it would have been much more so.

I am sure I understand the principle of fruitfulness, as I never could have done by any other treatment. Let me try to explain it to you. The pear drops when it is ripe. Until that time, all your care and devotion, however necessary in promoting fermentation, cannot make it come, and then it comes in a moment of itself, spontaneously and irrepressibly. Now in the case of a Christian, ripeness means the result of a certain experience. What is that experience, and what is the indication of its having been completed, or of the pear being ripe? The experience consists in a struggle, by the care of digging, enriching, pruning, and fencing, to bring the tree onward, and to bring the fruit out. The result is attained when the *struggle ceases*—there can be no ripe fruit till the struggle ceases. I am far from meaning, that by voluntarily arresting the struggle, you can shorten the process which leads to maturity. The struggle is just as necessary to the progress of the Christian, as fermentation is necessary to the ripening of the pear—but as in the one case, the marked sign of maturity is the ceasing of fermentation, so in the other case, it is the ceasing of the active struggle. You must come to a state of true passivity.

What is this true passivity? Certainly nothing but the *maturity of faith*—the perfection of the principle, by which those who are united to Christ receive life and strength from Him—a full consciousness of our union, or that perfect communion with Him, as our Head, which is expressed in believing prayer. There is a perfect sympathy between the Head and the members—our life is in the Head—it is drawn thence by ceaseless prayer. But are not our prayers often more of a struggle to exercise the life supposed to be in us already, than a simple feeling of emptiness, and reliance on the Spirit of life in Christ Jesus, to fill us? We either do not know ourselves to be empty, or knowing it, we are not reconciled to such a condition. We struggle for *life in ourselves.* How plain it is, that a continuous flow of life from the fountain, and consequently fruit-bearing, are quite inconsistent with the struggle to dig out a new cistern, or to mend a broken one. Have you ever thought of the deep meaning of the words, "Without me ye can do nothing?"

Is not this what we want, to come into closer communion with Him? It is not any clearer knowledge of God, or of Christ, or of sin, or of duty, or of the way of salvation—it is more than any of these, that we want. As a member of the body out of correspondence with the head is dead, to rise above that death which is constantly dragging us downward, to come into full constant overflowing communion with our Head, is not that all we need for life, for progress, for fruitfulness, for the spirit of self-sacrifice, for lost humanity? Then will our own desire be, through the short remainder of our lives, to do nothing else but think every day and every hour what we can do to testify our love to Him.

And now as to your own case, my dear friend, be assured it is simply this, God has *chosen* you to sanctification. I know this by the double sign of his inward, and his outward, dealings with you—and by sanctification I mean the purification of your affections. And those new affections, which will subjugate the old, can only be produced by the more full revelation (through the Spirit) of Christ's (your Head) affection for you. How full the New Testament is of the promise of the Spirit! It is the great promise; and what is the promise of the Spirit? "He shall take of the things of Christ and show them unto us." The promise of the Spirit, is practically a promise that Christ will so reveal His love to us, and in us, that all wrong affections shall be completely subjugated. You do not doubt the promise of the blood, nor its efficiency for pardon, why doubt the promise of the Spirit and its efficacy for purification? in the fulfillment of which, Christ will "manifest Himself unto you," "come to you," "take up His abode with you;" in virtue of which, "you shall ask what ye will and it shall be done unto you;" in virtue of which you shall abide in His love as He abides in His Father's love—and His joy shall remain in you;—in virtue of which, by the close and constant communion with Christ, of whom we are members of His body, of His flesh, and of His bones, the germ of your sanctification shall grow to perfection. * * * * * It is my daily joy and theme of thanksgiving, that you have got so far on—that you have passed probably, I may say, I think, certainly, the only serious difficulties. In a little while you shall be "filled with the fullness of God." What a promise! * * * * * Since I have had a being, I have never had such unmingled, elevated, and almost ecstatic happiness as for a week past. I am up in the highest region of breathing mortal air—but I am drawing you with me.

XIV.

WITH desire have I desired the time to come, when I should once more enjoy the privilege of a free hour with the man of my heart. I must write something to you now, small as it may be, both in bulk and weight, about Maurice's Essays, which I have read, and re-read, and mean to read again, thinking of you all the time, much wondering what would be the effect of his views upon your mind. I wish now to describe to you their effect upon mine—though perhaps I ought to postpone writing till I have thought still farther.

I must first say that this man, Maurice, carried me entirely away at first by his show of qualities which among theologians are rare—his talking always to the heart, and yet always through the understanding; but particularly by his most ingenious, and in some instances successful, efforts to harmonize and almost identify the dogmas of the Church with the demands of our nature, as uttered blindly through heathen philosophies and superstitions (of which more hereafter), to say nothing of his powers as a writer and thinker, his affluent yet simple diction, his masterly ease, the great compass of his thoughts, and the fullness of his sympathy with man. By traits like these he really carried me away. I was ready, and sometimes but too happy, to cast in my lot with him. At present, however, I am quite of another mind. I have no doubt, indeed, but he is unsound according to any orthodox standard. But I certainly look upon him as a Christian, and surely a most accomplished man.

I think I have a very clear view of the root of all his errors. The end of all his refinement is to vindicate and magnify the love of God. But he does this by virtually denying the Divine holiness—by shutting his eyes to the worst effect of sin, and that in which the evil nature especially appears, viz.: the wound which it inflicts on God's moral sensibilities, which is the cause of his wrath against it. The whole evil of sin, as Maurice views it, appears in its natural (not its judicial) effect upon the mind of the sinner; its only effect upon the mind of God is to excite His pity.

Occasionally an expression may occur which intimates more, but it is meant evidently to conciliate Orthodoxy, and in any deep sense is repudiated by his system. I cannot learn from him that God hates sin with a perfect hatred. It grieves Him as the transgression of a child grieves a parent, but it does not provoke Him to threaten it in good earnest with everlasting punishment. On the contrary, the only effect of sin on God, as far as I can learn from Maurice, is to bring out in all its intensity His love to man. Love, according to Maurice, is comprehensive of holiness. They cannot be distinguished. The very holiness of God, therefore, obliges Him to save man from the effects of sin.

And how is this done? See Maurice, page 49, and his doctrine expanded in that and subsequent chapters. According to him, all are righteous in the *Righteous One*, for all are in Him, or, which with Maurice is the same thing, He is in all, in one not less than another. What is the proof of this? The flimsiest that I ever saw adduced for a position so important, drawn from a particular interpretation, or I may say perversion of the experience of Job, which by an assumption still more glaring the writer asserts, p. 47, to be the experience of universal humanity. It rests absolutely on the amazing assumption that every man, of every class, from the most contented Pharisee to the miserable malefactor, possesses, and in given circumstances always becomes conscious of a righteousness which is deeper and stronger than his sin—a righteousness derived from his union with the Righteous One, in all whose redeeming acts all are alike interested. On the way in which this redemption becomes effectual he speaks only in general. But that the result of his system, or of his principles, is a refined universalism there can be no doubt. In his last essay he is forced to confess it, for what else can he mean by the middle paragraph on page 360?

Though I have always held that the system which makes love more prominent than wrath is the best system for men of all classes, and though, if I felt as Maurice does, that there was no other ground but the one he takes, on which the *depth and sincerity of God's love* could be vindicated, I might go over to his side. This is far, however, from being my mind.

My grand objection to the system of Maurice is, that by divesting sin of its worst aspect, it robs the love of God of its highest and most peculiar manifestation. If I did not believe that the holiness of God was something which could be distinguished from His love, something in virtue of which He hated sin, and was bent upon its punishment, with the same intense sincerity with which, in virtue of His love, He pities the sinner, and is bent upon his deliverance, it seems to me that neither my misery as a subject of wrath, nor God's love in giving His Son, nor Christ's agony to save me, would have the same effect upon my heart and conscience which they have now. I should feel that my heart was defrauded, as well as my conscience.

You will observe, that Maurice has no conception of any relation between God and man but that of father and child. But do men—while they are sinning, and intending to sin, look upon God as their Father? Suppose, however, to give the greater force to this particular view, that God *is* their Father. Is He nothing but a father? Does not every child know that the parent is also a man, and that, as such, he is governed by other affections than love to his offspring—that behind the love which beams in his paternal face, and awakens only joy and happiness, there are other qualities which are calculated to awaken fear? that the love of his offspring, however strong in the paternal breast, is not so strong as the love of truth and honor and integrity, and that in case of a conflict between the social bond and the bond of moral principle, there is an end of the blessed relation? And is not this what every thoroughly convicted sinner feels, viz., that the love of the Father has been supplanted by the workings of the other principles of His moral nature?

I shall have to stop now rather abruptly. Accept the above as a beginning. If well, as I now am, and other things favor, I should like to say some things more. I do want to say one thing now, however. I do assure you, my dear brother, that I feel daily that there has never lived a man on earth whose condemnation at the day of judgment is more certain than mine, if the *righteousness of Christ*, in which alone I trust, is not an all-sufficient protection. I am more and more reduced to the necessity of depending on Christ alone for justification and eternal life, or yielding entirely to despair. But I do assure you, also, that I have now such a confidence in my being destined in a little while to feel the embrace of those hands which were pierced for me, that the assaults of a doubting conscience hardly move me —and thus, I believe, it is with you.

Let us rejoice; yea, sing for joy, as we do,

blessed be our Rock· "My soul doth magnify the Lord, my spirit hath rejoiced in *God my Saviour*."

XV.

As, in a voyage of discovery, the ship which first comes in sight of land holds out a signal to its comrades to cheer them on, so you will believe me when I tell you that, deep beyond all earthly enjoyment is my happiness in assuring you that the port of Heaven is in sight, and that you shall soon certainly see it! Commonly, we are moored to a little island, (or if unmoored for a moment never get out of sight of it,) which to the eye of self seems a continent at least, if not the universe. But of late I have come very near an experience, if I have not quite reached it, which I am sure is the goal of all my struggles—the absorption of self in God, rest from selfish inquietude, infinite satisfaction in God.

Is not the great impeding element which prevents our progress heavenward our desire to think well of *ourselves?* which, if there were a basis for it in our characters, if we were angels, for example, (though I apprehend the angels are so absorbed in thoughts of God that they do not have a thought about themselves,) would be all right; but, in such as we actually are, it is simply pride. Can you not see that your desires for sanctification, and your efforts for it, and the pain arising from your failures, spring, in a great degree, from the desire to stand well in your own estimation? that what you want is not righteousness merely, but a *self*-righteousness?

Now it is certainly a great part of God's dealings with us to destroy entirely the principle of pride or self-esteem; and yet it is equally certain that His purpose or desire in regard to us is, that we shall be *saints*—truly exalted. One great end in the Gospel plan, its chief end so far as we are concerned, is our sanctification. And the peculiarity of the Gospel plan is that it eventually effects this in such a way as completely precludes self-righteousness, and, of course, pride and vanity.

Sanctification may be almost defined as self-forgetfulness or self-abandonment. I do not attach much importance to that constitutional sympathy with beings of our own nature, which makes us in a sense self-forgetting. This makes one amiable, but not truly holy. Holiness is that self-forgetting which is inspired by absorbing thoughts of God—a rise above the plane of self by absorbing views of His fullness of love, glory and beauty. It is our unceasing reference to the glory of self, instead of the glory of God—our extreme self-love, which appears even in our desires for holiness and in our acts of duty, which constitutes the essence of our sinfulness—the law of sin in our nature. Sanctification is the breaking up of this law—the turning away our thoughts and affections entirely from self, and placing them supremely, and at length wholly, on God.

How can this be done but by God's presenting Himself to us in such a manner that (sinners, deeply and hopelessly sinners as we are) we shall no more have any occasion for a single selfish care, desire, or emotion. Suppose He had told us simply that He wanted us to be holy, and that He never would be pleased with us until we were holy, or only in so far as we were holy. You may be sure that the Gospel method is just the opposite of that, for that would make deliverance from self hopeless.

What is the Gospel method? "Who of God"—that is by God's purpose or appointment—"is made unto us sanctification." Sanctification in the case of the angels, as well as in ours, is dependent on justification. The angels can keep themselves holy, that is, untainted by self-regard and absorbed in God, only while they feel that God has nothing against them, but, on the contrary, entirely loves them. Faith in God's perfect, changeless love to them, secures their perfect and changeless love to Him—not as a motive, which would suppose them to be mercenary, but from the law of creaturely dependence.

Christ, then, becomes our sanctification essentially by being our righteousness—practically or experimentally in virtue of our trusting His righteousness, which not only relieves us from all selfish care about sin, but fills us with the love of God. When you have such a faith in His righteousness as delivers you from all dread of going into the presence of God, from all feeling that you have to be or do something different from what you are, or are doing, to be entitled to the right of a beloved, accepted child, your sanctification is begun. You have no conception now of the manner in which God will draw you and reveal His love to you after, by your present course of experience, you have been humbled out of all self-estimation. Without this previous process the other cannot be, but it is just as certain to succeed it as the summer to follow the winter.

I never experienced before such a rest of heart (that *tired* member), a rest which is as perfect as I can hope will be at all permanent till I pass the swellings of Jordan; if that can be called a rest which evokes the highest mental and spiritual action. It will give you pleasure to know that I have what I consider a special Divine guidance in my work. Without this (which has long been the subject of my prayer) I could not have gone on at all. Providence, however, is very mysterious, and I cannot be sure that the great help I am receiving this winter may not be a preparation for my departure from the world. Of one thing I am sure, that the great condition of the successful performance of my work lies in my making such a real surrender of all my plans and desires not only in reference to life in general, but particularly in reference to this the most promising work of my life (my Isaac, I may call it), that if I should be laid aside by disease, or summoned suddenly to the other world, I may, like Abraham, obey.

That the new year upon which we are entering may be made a happy one to both of us, living or dying, by Christ's nearer presence, is my prayer.

XVI.

* * * * * I NEVER was more earnestly engaged in my peculiar studies—all bearing upon one object—the clearest solution for my own benefit, and the simplest description for that of others, of the nature and method of sanctification. Relations of thought which never entered my mind before, perfectly inspire, without in the least bewildering me. They are the harvest from a seed long buried.

I told you in my last letter, that I would let you know when I had reached a certain "summit" I was trying to scale. My own state for several years has been one of assured conviction that everything in my salvation and sanctification depended simply on the faithfulness of God, which was itself secured by the vicarious work of Christ in respect to all who were truly united to Him—that is, who truly believed, trusted, and depended on Him; and that my whole duty lay in constantly assuring myself that Christ was my Saviour, and could not fail, against all appearances to the contrary.

The effect of this assumption (for which, though I call it so, I had the strongest scriptural as well as experimental warrant) is gradually, but most indistinctly and unceasingly, opening my soul, if I may so speak, to the embrace of Divine love, and thus in deadening my worldly sensibilities, from the power of which I had suffered so much, was very marked, until at length I began to feel assured that the great deliverance was accomplished—that the seed which could not be destroyed was in me, and that however imperfect my sanctification at present, my perfect victory over all enemies and through all trials was secured by a purpose which could not be frustrated.

But while personally delivered, I have been enduring a great struggle for the deliverance of others. Death, connected as it now is with an assurance of Heaven, would be welcome, I trust, at any time, but for the hope which I have had of saying a word on the subject of sanctification, which shall strike off the chains from many captive souls. My hope of doing it is strong—the hope of really delivering the message which has so long been inwardly consuming me; and yet, my real concern is not about the issue of my labor, but simply about my daily duty. I am thrown into an arena of conflict where my duty is to fight, whatever may be the result; a fight not with flesh and blood, not even with my own flesh at length, so much as with the great enemy. My intellectual labor, inspired first by my own deep necessities, if it is worth anything, will penetrate one of his strongholds; and my duty is to go on though earth and hell are moved to oppose me, which I can only do by obtaining new strength from above. If my life and health are preserved, I have no reason to doubt of my success; and at length I am enabled to pray for success simply and wholly on account of the interest which other souls have in it. For myself, it matters not, if I only fight on. If Death takes me while thus engaged, I shall be able to say, "Thrice welcome."

My recent experience—which I call a "summit"—differed from others which I have often had only in the greater clearness of its revelations. The substance of these revelations has been always the same—the depths and breadths of Divine love.

I never received a letter from you which gave me greater encouragement than your last, in my efforts to guide you, as far as I have been guided myself, into the mystery of fellowship with God. Pray continually for a clearer vision of His love. The truth is, the manifestation of God's love, as contained in the Gospel, is perfect—the whole difficulty lies in our vision. Open your eyes, open your heart, till His love and light flood your whole being. This, and this only, will ensure the full development, and ultimate perfection, of the "incorruptible seed" of Grace which has surely been planted there; and once planted, it can never be rooted up, nor fatally obstructed. However feeble in the beginning, it will grow and expand till (time being allowed for the operation) it has uprooted and cast out whatever is opposed to it. It will be always gaining, while the other will be always losing (even when it seems to be gaining), however slowly and insensibly.

This is made sure by the relation of the regenerate soul to Christ, and the nature of the covenant of Grace. In this sense, the love of God is stronger in the feeblest Christian than all worldly affections, which often seem to be sensibly or consciously the stronger. The great proof of its existence in many cases is the ingenuous pain which such failures cause the regenerate. Notwithstanding their failures they still fight, and mean to fight all their days. If the enemy conquers, it is against their will and their endeavors, and they do not relinquish the hope of ultimate sanctification, or clear deliverance from inward evil.

Plant yourself, my dear friend, on this foundation—God's love and faithfulness to His covenant of Grace. Hold it fast against earth and hell, and in a little while " your enemies will be found liars unto you, and you shall tread upon their high places." Keep to the Scriptures—think only of Christ's words; never mind your actual present inward state while you are conscious of believing in Christ's love, and trying to obey His commands.

With a sympathy which shall ever increase till we meet in glory. Your friend.

XVII.

I OUGHT not to write any more, for I have been writing through the morning, until the state of my head admonishes me to desist; and yet I have that to say which ought to give you great encouragement. Where sin hath abounded, Grace shall much more abound. None but a poor undone creature, who feels himself abandoned, or worthy to be abandoned, by the whole creation, can know God's real *nature*. I often wonder that you make so little of the book of Psalms. I have found such comfort in the devotional exercises of David lately as words cannot express. In no other parts of the Scriptures is the *benignity* of the Divine nature made so apparent to me—particularly his confession.

If I ever write a book, the object of it shall be to show that by the holiness of God, as that term is used in the Psalms, and elsewhere generally in the Old Testament, is meant mainly His infinite elevation above all those human passions which are the opposite of love. His forgiveness of sin to such an extent, is especially the effect of His holiness in this sense. His forgiving it through a propitiation only illustrates the same thing—for "herein was the *love* of God manifested"—herein was its highest manifestation, "that He gave His Son to be a propitiation for our sins.

Suppose we believe that God is Love, which is

the whole Gospel—believe it first in regard to all humanity—believe, through all appearances to the contrary, that the vindication of God's love must be the end of the mystery of man—believe it especially, and every moment, with respect to ourselves, for which we know the warrant to be such that, without this basis, there can be no duty; suppose we believe, also, that being "risen with Christ," life is no longer in any sense a probation, but simply a redemption, a rising higher and higher toward the perfect stature of spiritual manhood—believe that it is God's end in every, even the minutest event of our daily life, to confer upon us the true happiness which can only be found in the voluntary acceptance of God's will in place of our own, —that this is especially the end of all His dealings with us—the destruction of self-will—by which the sense of a life in self shall be constantly changing into the consciousness of a life in God. This, and nothing short of this, is what the Gospel declares and promises.

I take it, that the peculiar condition of Eternity is, that the sense of self is, in that state, completely lost in the consciousness of God—not that self is destroyed, or ceases to exist, but is forgotten, lost sight of, in the consciousness of a Higher Presence. And may not that be our condition now, germinally at least, and that germ constantly expanding? What makes our life a cold shadow, what prevents its being all sunshine, but an obstinate self-will interposing between us and the Father of our spirits? Is not that a Gospel indeed, which "abolishes death," the only barrier between time and eternity, and by its doctrine of love destroys the only barrier, self-love, which prevents our union with God? "O, the depth of the riches of the wisdom of God!" This is the Gospel, my child, which God has commissioned me with. He bids me say to you, that your life is "hid with Christ in God." Henceforth you have simply to seek it *there*—no more as of old, in probationary self-efforts, and self-corrections, from which you have "risen." The life is already legally yours, "reserved for you in Heaven." The knowledge of this is the great point gained.

Perhaps you read a late account of some English travelers in the Alps, who were tied together by the same rope, so that though some were in advance of others, the last were as sure as the first of reaching the top. In that case, the rope broke, and the weaker ones went down the precipice. But ours cannot break for it is fastened within the vail. If I should first ascend to God, one of my sweetest thoughts will be that you are following in the same path, and perhaps are helped a little over the roughnesses of the upward way by the known experience of your humble teacher and forerunner.

Very sure am I, that if I get first to the heights of victory (eternal), I shall, if such a thing be possible, stretch down a long arm to pull you up to me! * * * * * To know that you now feel that "*not* to trust Christ is presumption," instead of the contrary, repays me for all my care. You have no idea what a change similar to this will occur in all your conceptions of God, and His ways with men.

XVIII.

I SEIZE the first moments of my release from a long intellectual captivity, to say something in reply to your kind letters. Though under some disadvantages for writing from a state of physical exhaustion greater, I think, than I ever knew before, my nature will not suffer me to rest until

I have paid at least a small instalment upon the debt which the free expression of your confidence has laid upon me; and in one sense I can do it easily, for though the flesh is weak, the spirit never before was so willing.

After a life's struggle, I am standing now on the same "Delectable Mountains," with the atmosphere of which your late communications are so clearly impregnated. I am surveying, without an intervening cloud, those everlasting possessions, the certainty of our attaining which seems now (after long endurance) to be equally realized by both of us. I need not say how much it added to my bliss to hear your voice so near me, and to meet you again, after so long a separation by paths hid from each other, in these suburbs of the Celestial City.

The sole point to which I would devote my letter is the ground of our certainty, which is either objective or subjective. Of the first (the love of Christ), I need say nothing. It is unchangeable; and of the other (our love to Him), I have only to say, it will last just as long as, by a perfect faith *in His love to us*, we maintain an increasingly vigorous conflict with the selfishness of our nature, or strive to be like Him. I cannot see in particular what trials are before me, but I know that from one cause, if from no other, such a life as I am now enjoying must be vulnerable. The malice of Satan will not allow me any absolute rest. The adversary will seek to impair the sense of union with my God, even though knowing that he cannot entirely divide us; because it is only in so far as we retain the sense of union with Christ that we can glorify Him by our fruit; therefore, Satan will ever aim to weaken that, though he can go no farther. I do feel that I have an enemy in him, of whose power I have not always had the same distinct impression as now. In other ways, however, which I have not time nor strength at present to explain, I find this knowledge of Satan a solution of some of my worst difficulties. * * * * * Is it not plain that all our inefficiency as Christians has arisen from the want of assurance that Christ and we were one—had but one interest? To come into full, constant, overflowing communion with our Head, particularly in the spirit of self-sacrifice for lost humanity, is not this the consuming desire of our hearts?

I trust that my views are entirely settled at last in regard to the distinction between the outward and inward life. My only dread is lest any partial success in the outward part of the struggle (the performance of outward duties) may make the inward life less earnest. What I *am* before God is, after all, the great question, not what I *do*, except as this latter shows what I am. I have no doubt that this is exactly according to the will of God—that what he asks of us is the inward sacrifice. In proportion as that is rendered the fruit will appear in the life, but much more likely in the manner of doing ordinary things than in any special manifestations. My fear at present is all directed against the indulgence of any desire not prompted by or consistent with a consciousness of the supremacy of Christ in my soul—the non-realization of His presence and will in every event that may happen to me. This causes me to shrink from certain possible conditions of life; and yet I do not mean that I am at present under any alarm, for my sense of God's immeasurable and unchangeable love forbids it. * * * * * Have you read "Ecce Deus?" I have read it, every word consecutively, though I never spent so long a time reading a book of its size, having to read chapter after chapter and page after page several times before I could get forward. Of all the books which I have read in ten years, so many and so original, on the same subject, none bears a comparison with it for union of intellectual depth and comprehensive knowledge with spiritual insight and fervor; for showing up the spirit of the age, and just where the Church stands, what her disease is, and what the remedy is; and for a plain, almost impromptu way of expressing his convictions.

One thing, doubtless, which makes me such a devotee to the book is finding that its most cardinal principle is the identical one which has interested me so peculiarly in my studies for months past—the true idea of the Father. * * * * * When I said to you that you ought to spend much time in study, I did not mean that you should give yourself to *great sermons.* I must frankly tell you that I fear you will find a snare there. Above all other things I advise you to walk humbly. Let nothing tempt you to go beyond your measure. O, could I live my youth over again! The difficulty with me was simply that though Christ was in my head He was not deeply enough in my heart. Our work is to preach Christ, and this is an impossibility if He is not our *Life*. How I prayed for you this morning!

XIX.

MONTHS ago I had a long letter for you in my head, which was detained there by other drafts upon that organ, and more recently, by some incapacity in the organ itself for honoring any drafts upon it. I have felt myself your "debtor" ever since I heard those sad words from you, to the effect that after "twenty years" of struggle with self, you could not see that any advantage had been gained, except that your religion (by which, I suppose, you meant your sense of sin) had gained a little more reality; perhaps you meant, that your belief in the *need* of redemption had become somewhat like your sense of natural wants.

The words did not make me sad on your account. I call them so, only because they came from a heavy heart, and were uttered with a sad expression of countenance. My own thoughts were—

here is a soul in training for a great mercy sooner or later. The only reason of all your sorrows, failures, and trials is, that, as light would not be appreciated without an experience of darkness, so God's love in our redemption cannot be known, that is, *revealed in us*—cannot be the subject of an inward realization, but in proportion to the experience we have had of heart-misery in sin.

I have had an experience lately of sorrow being turned into joy, which, hoping it may encourage your hopes, and strengthen your determination to keep "struggling on," I will tell you of. The trouble in my head, which when I saw you I hoped was passing away, is now pronounced by all physicians to be a nervous derangement, which, to say the least, is alarming enough to make one serious. There is certainly no natural prospect, as far as I can see or learn, of a speedy change for the better.

The moral effect has been, of course, to make me generally very, very thoughtful. Prayer has been a simple, but O, how earnest a talk with the Preserver of men, asking him not for life, but for *light*, that I might see my spiritual position. Not to be saved from temporal death, though I have had so much reason to apprehend it, but to be delivered from all spiritual disabilities has been my cry—to be cleansed—to be saved from my prevailing sins hereafter, either by death transferring me to another world, or by grace constraining and governing my life in this.

And how graciously has the Lord hearkened unto the voice of my supplications. Direful as has been my case in its outward aspect, it has inclosed the sweetest drop of Divine joy I have ever received. The fiercest trial has passed over me without leaving a singe. I have been not only submissive, but full of joy, arising from the conviction that God's hand of love was ministering the cup which should infuse into me a new power of holiness.

For a long time I have been conscious of wanting holiness, but no words can express to you how dim have been my views of what I wanted under the name of holiness. It was an advance upon my former state, in which the highest idea I had of spiritual blessedness was to have the favor of God—to have his anger (by virtue of the Atonement) turned to favor, was about my whole desire before, though not my whole theoretic notion of salvation.

Then I began to desire something else, but something of which I had a very dim perception. I called it holiness, but it was not what I mean by holiness now, though it might have been the germ of it. It was a desire for the *enjoyment* of God more than for *conformity* to Him. Still it was much more than a desire for His favor. What I wanted was a principle or character which would not only make me pleasing to God, but which would make Him in His whole perfection (and not in His mercy merely) pleasing to me—so that I could have perfect communion with Him, and the enjoyment arising from such communion. This has been my real end for some years past. "As the hart panteth after the water brooks," so has my soul, I may say, daily and with growing earnestness, "panted after God." But, still, it has not been so much to honor and glorify God as to enjoy Him. Perhaps there is not a great deal in this distinction. I can say now, however, that my desire to glorify God, not before men (desirable as that is), but in the thoughts of my heart, is very distinctly stronger than to enjoy Him. No passion that I have ever had has exercised me as my desire to have God's will consume mine, which is what I now mean by holiness.

For some weeks previous to the beginning of this month I had been "breathing out threatening and slaughter" against —— *self.* I was willing to die a martyr's death if I could get rid of that cursed thing that separated between me and God. Just at that time the trouble in my head began, and soon increased with such violence that my agony, for many days, was extreme. Now what I want to say is, that it was in the midst of this anguish that I got my first thoroughly-true idea of the nature of holiness, and my first experience of perfect bliss. Though but a drop, it was as pure as anything ever known in Heaven—it was just what they have in Heaven—they can have nothing beyond it except in measure. I have often wanted to die that I might know something of the nature of heavenly blessedness. I shall never have that desire again, for that reason, at least; but O! how willingly I could have died at that moment, that the drop might become a perennial stream! "If it be possible, let this cup pass from Me. Nevertheless, *not My will*, but *Thine*, be done—*not* my will, but *Thine!*"

Dear friend, when you come to that, while in the most miserable outward condition, you will have reached the end of that dark and toilsome way you are now traveling; and you will reach it. If a failure had been possible, I should have failed. No religious life has ever been retarded by greater embarrassments, no religious experience ever more corrupted by earthly elements; so corrupt still, that I can do right in nothing except by an Invisible Power, which (insensibly for the most part to myself) is according to His immutable promise working in me.

I will not give you reason for blaming me, as I have just been blaming my doctor, for not telling me at the beginning, as he might have done, precisely the course which my disease would take, and the final result of it. I will not leave you to guess how your trouble is to end. The Apostle Paul knew nothing better of his Philippian and Thessalonian brethren than I know of you. He knew, upon possibly less evidence than I have in your case, that God had begun a good work in them; how very imperfect the work was, is manifest enough from sundry of his cautions. But with the impression which his own experience had given him of the goodness, and gentleness, and faithfulness of Christ, he had no hesitation in assuring them that the love which had commenced the work would surely finish it; and that they had nothing at all to do but just in reliance upon God's care, and certain promises of help, all sufficient in the hour of need, to go on, "rejoicing in hope, patient in tribulation, continuing instant in prayer," in everything without carefulness. This is the only way to render a suitable and an acceptable recompense for His love and grace.

If you were just beginning the Christian life I might be a little more cautious. But in the case of one who has kept her face Christ-ward, or rather God-ward, for twenty years, who, though deploring her want of progress in that time, has not gone back, and has no idea of doing so, the Spirit tells me to cry, "Comfort ye, comfort ye my people." "Say unto her that her warfare is accomplished, that her iniquity is pardoned,"—her redemption is nigh—"Behold I come quickly."

You will find a marvelous strictness of truth in all that "quickly" means. Our Lord's coming seems slow to us, because we are children. Three weeks to a child who is expecting his good things at Christmas holidays, seems an age. But when your days of rejoicing have come, your only wonder, when you consider their glory, will be how they could have come so soon.

In respect to my health, I know not what a day may bring forth. I have had no pain, indeed, for nearly a week, but one constant dull pressure in my head, scarcely intermitted for one waking moment. But O, what peace—what joy and freedom in prayer,—what a clear apprehension of the truths of Grace,—what expectations of, as well as aspirations after a complete deliverance from the power of sin, and a perfect union with Christ,—what an all-conquering sense of the Divine love and of the beatitude involved in perfected holiness: I feel almost willing to go straight through death in the hope of at once reaching it.

* * * * *

[The fragments of letters which follow were written by Mr. James after his physical pain and weakness had become very great—so extreme that he could write but a few lines, in pencil, at a time, and those more and more faintly and tremulously traced, as while the spirit was growing strong for its emancipation, the earthly tabernacle was dissolving.]

LAST WORDS.

It was in my last letter to you, I think, that I spoke about hardly being able to realize that I was mortal, so established seemed my health. I can now tell you a better story than that a great deal. Things have occurred since that letter which make it certain that physical suffering is to be my portion for months to come; but with it, and through it there has come such an enlargement of spiritual (immortal) vision, that I am blessing God for my pains as I never did before for the highest and choicest of His gifts.

If you will read the chapter on Prayer in Dora Greenwell's 'Essays, which I send you, you will understand perfectly the state of my soul. The prayer which she describes has been the character of my prayers for some time—when I was in perfect health apparently; and I perfectly understand how this state of suffering is intended to bring me more thoroughly into the state of union with God, which these prayers simply contemplated. I have not the shadow of doubt about it, and if my doctor had said, "This condition of yours means death," as for a time I understood him to mean, my faith would have only been the more exalted.

Now, my dear friend, I say these things to you about myself, because in my experience you have a perfect pledge of your own glorious triumph. In your last letter, what most struck me was your lament that you could not rise to the higher world. I did not understand a desire to die, but to have Heaven come down to you here. In my next, I hope I may have strength to reveal the way of living in Heaven while here on earth, as I never could before.

I have to write in great haste, as I cannot sit up for an hour without great pain. My work on sanctification is more certain than ever, if possible—life continuing, and my enthusiasm in it is constantly rising. You will see the drift of my thoughts, somewhat, in "Ecce Deus," which I send you, with Dora Greenwell's book—especially in the chapter on the cross of Christ. No book that I ever read yet, is so much in the spirit of my thoughts as connected with my present work.

* * * * * Nothing you ever wrote made me more thankful than what you said in your last—of the sweetness of your late experience. I ex-

pect, if I live, to see you so far advanced in holiness, that Divine enjoyment of a higher kind than you have ever known will be your general state—a position from which you will look back with wonder on the days when, although God was just as near to you as He ever could be in all the beauty and sweetness of a personal love, something—hardly a thing—a mere illusion obscured your vision so that you could not behold Him. How plain it is to me, that God has been in all our past, and is leading us to a "city of habitation." Fear not—only believe.

* * * * * Though I carry in myself the sentence of death I am in the enjoyment of more peace than, as my friend Dr. Spencer, of Brooklyn, said, in his last hours, such a sinner is worthy of. The whole Gospel to me now is the "flesh of the Son of God." This is the bread which sustains my famishing soul. I see plainly that the Law dooms me to death. I not only see it with my understanding, I feel it in all my nature. Sin has separated me from God—this is death. That Christ died this very death of separation from God for me, that I might be saved from it—that He gave His life for mine, this is the Gospel to me. This sen-

sation, or experience of death which I endure, is nothing but the fellowship of His sufferings; and as I am crucified and buried with Him, I shall also live and reign with Him. This sense of my own death prompts me to such a dependence upon His death and sufferings for me, that I may be said, without exaggeration, to "eat His flesh." I lay hold of the flesh, the sacrifice, the *sin-offering* contained in the condemned flesh of Christ, as one famishing with hunger lays hold of bread; and it is my faith that as certainly as I thus eat His flesh I must partake of that life with which such an act is connected, by the promise of God; as certainly as through the law I die with Him, I shall be identified with Him in His resurrection.

* * * * * I am in a heaven of hope, yet never more pressed with what for want of a better term I must call trial. By which I mean, however, anything but suffering; the trial of suspended expectation, not knowing what may come next—possibly death, perhaps a lower deep of suffering before reaching it. Whatever is God's will, I wait but the word to sink or to soar; for height and depth are the same when assured neither of them, nor any other created thing can

separate us from the love of God which is in Christ Jesus our Lord.

* * * * * How I long to communicate myself to you, as I so often have before—but my weakness continues very great, and of the volume which I would like to convey to you I can give you but a leaf. O, could I, my friend, give you, and such as you, a tithe of the comfort and inward peace I feel! And yet, by no language could I give you all the sense of humiliation which I feel in reflecting upon my own past. My assurance is founded not at all upon "evidences," but upon the wonderfully strong idea I have of Grace. Seeing how plain it is, from the Scriptures, that one of God's ends, and perhaps His highest, is to magnify His grace, I cannot understand how one who hangs upon it, as I find myself compelled to do, can possibly be lost, and in this assurance "the new song" is begun.

I feel daily that death will certainly be my glorification—that is, the complete development of that union with Christ which has been begun here by a partial, and will be finished there by a perfect apprehension or vision of His glory.

* * * * * I write from the lounge in my

study, on which, between sitting and lying, I spend now the twelve hours of daylight. My actual condition is just what it was one month ago, but I have learned to bear it better, and that I have sometimes mistaken for a physical improvement. But my body is the Lord's. If He has any further use for it, in time He will find ways of making it sound again, or sufficiently so for those uses. I have had a blessed meditation on Psalm cxxxix. 13–17.

My spirits never were better. I have yet some hope from medical skill, though little ; but the inward man waxes stronger and stronger. I am sorry that my letter to Mr. N.——— gave you any gloomy impression, as, if I understand your letter, it did. I was far enough from gloom when I wrote it, and such is my ordinary state, gathering new strength from every indication that the time of my sojourning here is short.

I am delighted to hear of the improvement in your own health, and with a higher joy I think I discover some improvement in your faith. O, my friend, if you can once get established in the idea that your salvation is now certain—certain in virtue of Christ's love to you, to which all your own future efforts could never make the slightest addition, you will go forward at a very different pace from that of past years, and I have something for you which I think will give you this certainty, or show you exactly how it is attained, as very few things you have ever read have been able to do. You will soon receive four volumes, entitled "Waymarks in the Wilderness," a compilation of essays, by the Rev. Mr. Inglis, the editor of *The Witness,* which will put a knowledge of the Gospel into you which you never have had hitherto. I cannot answer for all of them, for I have read it only in small part, but in my next note, I will tell you what to read first.

Do you see *Hours at Home?* I sent for the number which was advertised to contain Dr. Bushnell's article on the "Moral Uses of Physical Pain," a most masterly production. Tired as I am, I must quote one passage which I know to be true. "There is nothing in all our experience that changes so many aspects of things and is so grandly productive and fertile of good. It is God's mute prophet in the body, giving there its mighty oracles to the soul."

Very sure I am, that while I trust in God's

mercy, I find even a greater satisfaction in being submissive to his will. I feel a cheerful confidence that whatever may be the outward event of this trial, it is meant to answer my prayer for holiness, and I do feel a pleasure, even in my sharpest pains, from hoping that that is their end. How good it is to be able to think well of God in every affliction, and to know that the hand that sends it never did a wrong to the meanest creature. * * * * * * Since the day of pain of which I wrote last, which was soon completely subdued by God's blessing upon remedies, I have been wafted on smooth seas and with propitious gales toward the shining shore, as I have supposed. But a most unexpected and unintelligible improvement has been going on within a few days, to-day particularly, which excites the strangest thoughts. It may amount to little in the end, but it is most noticeable at present.

The denizens of the basement were startled this morning by what they thought a vision. But it turned out to be the master of the house, who went down, staff in hand, to put things in order there, after an absence of nearly four months. I remained there. however, only about five minutes, and reascended the two flights of stairs without difficulty or fatigue. Come, when you can, to see me, my friend.

* * * * * About the change to which I adverted in my last, I must call upon my imagination to give it its real meaning. Well, then,—I was being wafted, as I said, on the calmest seas, to the shining shore—looking out to see some bright herald waiting my arrival—when, suddenly, a voice seemed to come from the Great Pilot from within the vail: "Turn the helm earthward!" Immediately, all my earthly members became obedient to orders. Disease seemed vanishing—no pain—appetite keen as the air, and my voice singing Alleluia a little louder than when having nothing but health to inspire it. I had not asked for this, nor had I even desired it, except as a signal of high favor; and, since weakness and pain have returned, the sweet will of God has calmed every commotion. That has been my opiate through every hour of suffering. I would like to live, if it were His will, to help others in their Christian life; to understand, and to give to others, God's plan of sanctifying His people from foundation to top-stone has been my desire; but, for myself, I am more

ready than ever to take that "bound"—a bound from all the solicitudes of earth, and from all its corruptions, into the bosom of Infinite Love.

The certainty of that transition is just as sure to me as the Gospel itself, or as the being of God. "Heaven opens on my eyes—my ears with sounds seraphic ring;" and yet I feel myself to be the meanest, the most unworthy, of all who were ever with propriety called by Christ's sacred name. If you should hear, before long, that I am gone, believe, my dear friend, that while I am "resting in glory," I shall not be without far tenderer thought of you than I could ever have here—the friend whom I have left in this vale of conflict. How earnestly shall I still look forward to the time of your glorification, and, of course, with a desire (may I not say, a prayer?) for your deliverance from the machinations of evil, far stronger than I could feel here, where my knowledge was so imperfect. If I have prayed so much for you while encumbered with the imperfections of the flesh, how much more, when delivered from these incumbrances, shall I think of you as still bound by earth's fetters!

What joy your letters give me! Continue to

write to me. I never before was in a condition to appreciate fully the life-giving power of human sympathy. A thrill of pleasure runs through me every time I hear the door-bell ring, and the word brought up from some kind friend, to know how the sufferer is, or the request to see me. I mention this only to give you an idea of the comforting effect of your letters.

* * * * * I mean to give you a few lines once in a while, while I can, which I trust will be to the last week of my waning life. How I was cheered and revived by your visit! Whately inclines to the belief that the intermediate state is one of unconsciousness. I do not. But be that as it may, the great truth is sure. "We shall not all sleep, but we shall all be changed in a moment, in the twinkling of an eye, at the last trump." Then, if not before, our communion shall be renewed, never again to be broken.

I want you to thank our God, my dear friend, with me, that, in the hour of my deepest distress, He has been nearest to me. I have been full of spiritual comfort, even when racked with pain—and in the midst, too, of the clearest view of sin; my sins! my sins! But this only makes the voice of pardon more exquisitely soothing. God is making me to realize both the terrible nature of sin and the wondrous efficacy of atoning blood. He has given me perfect rest through an overwhelming expansion of the idea that Christ *died*—put His sacred body between the sinner and the curse, so that the severer the trial, the greater and surer the blessing to any one who just believes that simple truth. That is the light on which I fasten my eyes, and which fills me with hope while struggling, but not submerged, amidst the billows of eternity's ocean.

Good-bye, dear friend, with hope for your own health, and love (I never knew what it was to love before) to every friend whom I expect to meet in the land of everlasting rest.

* * * * * I write from my bed. My sufferings are very great, but my soul still rejoices in the broad sunlight; all my former experiences have been twilight compared with the present. While I live my love can never quit its hold of my dear earthly friends, and much less, I believe, after I have ascended. I cannot doubt that God is leading you in the same way in which He has been leading me. At the bottom of all is a desire for

purity, or a perfect conformity to God's will, which will not be denied. I have long wanted nothing else. To be such a debtor as I am to Grace, and yet to withhold anything from Him, seems to be the only thing I cannot endure. Therefore I just placed myself in His hands, that He might, by any means He chose to use, constrain the total relinquishment of self; and how has He done it? By bringing me into a trial in which self had no choice but to trust Him or perish, and then showing me that I had nothing to fear—that love belonged to Him just as light belongs to the sun—that it is all mine.

I would not exchange my sufferings, with the peace I have, for a diadem of stars.

* * * * * The *simplicity* of my confidence in God at present exceeds any ideal even, which I have had of such a state. I mention this to you partly to assuage your painful sympathies for me, and partly for your own encouragement. I wish I had strength to tell you fully the ground of my peace. For many months before this trouble came upon me, I enjoyed a higher degree of communion with God than ever before. To be like Him—to have the cursed root of sin eradicated, I offered

myself up in daily sacrifice; willing to suffer everything (for I saw plainly that it was only by suffering the end could be effected).

But with the first clear and real view of approaching judgment, all my *evidences* were of no more account than the drift-wood on which the drowning mariner tries to rest amidst the surges of the ocean. I saw myself as the basest of mankind; "of whom I am chief," became as easy as the alphabet. Still I felt as a child; quite as anxious that the Father, whom I had so injured, should be glorified, as that I should be delivered from His wrath; and now I fully appreciate, as I always had pretty well understood, the meaning of Christ's death. God glorified and my soul certainly saved by Christ's simply dying for me, without any reference to my own character, dying for my sins—a sense of which alone is necessary to get all the benefits of His death. I do not wonder that the only song in the upper world is: "To Him who hath loved us and washed us from our sins in His own blood; to Him be glory and dominion, forever and ever." Soon shall I join in that eternal song.

I wish I could tell you of the great mercy of

God to me in every respect. I suffer very little now except from weakness—and then the bright reflection from the world to which I am going! Everything indicates that the hand of a Father directs all things concerning me. Oh, the delightful repose that I had all last night! God do abundantly above all my thoughts and prayers for you, dear friend! * * * * * Since my last to you I have been gradually sinking; and it is evidently the impression of those around me, as it has long been my own, that there is no exit from my complicated malady but through the gate of death. I do not take the sofa of late nearly as much as formerly, and can read nothing of any-account. There is hardly a square inch of my body below the small of my back which is not the seat of pain. But I feel that it is sweet to suffer—to suffer anything from One in whose love I have such boundless confidence, and sure I am that all suffering from His hand is meant not only for my highest good but for my highest happiness. Anything ought to be sweet which binds us to the cross, and to the bosom of our only—in the purest and strongest sense—beloved, and fills the eye with Heaven. How natural, how, I might almost say, *human*, that Heaven seems as I approach its shores! It seems literally like going to the land of "green fields and still waters."

Never was there a person as low as I am, surrounded with more outward comforts; the best of nursing; the warmest sympathy of friends; delightful letters of affection—especially from ministers who have heard of my extremity. But infinitely better still, all is sunshine within. The tree is leafless, but the warm sun of Eternal Love is shining around me, and the two worlds seem to open into each other. The outward comforts I have are a small matter compared with the trust in my Heavenly Father, which flows on in a constant stream, no more to be shaken or changed than one's faith in the declarations of a father's love. God's Word, revealing his full character to me, is the fountain at which I quench my perpetual thirst for the knowlege of His love to me. I find this fountain not only free as water, but satisfying as water itself.

No young girl ever felt a more delightful fluttering in the prospect of a European tour, than I feel in the prospect of soon seeing the land of never-withering flowers, and of seeing Christ, and knowing Him, and being known of Him. If anything favorable occurs, you shall hear; if nothing, then farewell till we meet on the bank of the River of Life. In death as in life, yours,

W. J.

Here the pen drops from the hand which, even while faltering in death, was employed in expressing the love and faith of that great heart, and his undying desire to help others to gain the heights he himself had reached. Here, we will let another (from the letters connected with whose memorial of Mr. James we have already quoted) speak, believing that those who have followed this struggling yet victorious soul to the very gates of Glory, will like to linger and catch the last words of joy and triumph that fall from his lips as he enters in to be forever with the Lord.

EXTRACTS FROM

"VIEW OF MR. JAMES'S CHARACTER AND LIFE."

WRITTEN BY

Rev. Henry Neill.

* * * * * * Many may desire to know more about the natural stock, the early associations, the human traits of Mr. James. Born in Albany, New York, in 1797, his blood was a mixture of Irish and Dutch; Irish on the father's side, and Dutch on the mother's. He carried in himself the fire and sensibility of the one nation, with the depth and power of endurance in the other; an extraordinary and splendid combination. Withal he had a most vigorous physical constitution, a fine head, a glowing, warm, discerning, and expressive eye, a high and expansive forehead, a movement indicative of power and good breeding, and a presence that, by its elevation, frankness, and fearless-

ness, would vitalize an assembly before he spoke a word.

* * * * He was not self-conserving; he sought not his own preferment; he had to be frank by the regal type of his nature; he never assumed a posture or a tone; his manners were the undulation of his morals, and so identical with them, that, as with the old Romans, but one word, *mores*, was necessary to express both. His manners were the true exponent of his heart. The great organ of his nature was his heart; and this, like the ocean or the sun, was constantly distributing itself. * * * * And yet, who that saw him often, had any doubt that he held himself singularly indifferent to every form of natural bestowment and of external advantage (in which, also, he largely shared), by reason of a master passion of surpassing beauty and power, constantly working in him, even a never-ceasing desire to be in harmony with the Divine mind, in spirit and in movement? He panted after God, and assimilation to Him, in impulse and in action, as the hart panteth after the water-brooks. "I want holiness so much," he wrote, in a letter dated December, 1856, "that I might say I want nothing else. One additional

grain of holiness or conformity to God, with a consciousness that God was pleased with it, would outweigh a universe of every other kind of good."

This statement contains the key-note of his life. The desire expressed in it animated him at Princeton; led him to Dr. Gordon rather than to Chalmers, at Edinburgh; absorbed him at New York on his return from Scotland, when preaching to crowded assemblies from the pulpit made vacant by the death of Dr. John Mason; gave direction to his thoughts at Rochester, where he labored for many years, and since then has been ever revealing itself, in letters, in the selection of friends, in the choice of books, in themes for sermons, in essays, in conversations, in journeyings (for he never hesitated to travel a hundred miles to visit one whose doubts or fears he could not allay by his pen), in the language and tone of his devotions, never to be forgotten by any one who ever heard his words in prayer; until desire merged itself into a knowledge and enjoyment of God seldom granted in this world to the fallen sons of men. The unrest that at times appeared in him grew out of a sorrow often expressed and painfully active, that he was not, to his consciousness, perfectly "comformed to the image" of God's dear Son.

Greatly did many of his friends admire the type of his piety, in its deep undertone as well as in its strains of faith, and hope, and victory. He has revealed, in his letters, its nature, its sources, and its growth. * * * * * It is marvelous with what industry, cheerfulness, persistence, and fidelity, he gave himself to the work of correspondence with any one who he thought would receive and be benefited by his counsels. The labors of many men, on their sermons and in their parishes, were light, compared with the epistolary toils he voluntarily imposed upon himself, and, with delight, carried on year after year, through nearly a whole lifetime. Indeed, he has scarcely an acquaintance who is not in possession of many letters on progress in holiness, on the way to get rid of disturbing doubts, and to triumph over easily-besetting sins. From no painstaking did he shrink, could he only thus lift the burden from a suffering soul. Never did they that watch for the morning wait for the breaking of the day with half the anxiety that he did to see the shadows flee away from a clouded mind. And how he rejoiced when his hope was not disappointed! "The note of victorious faith, which rings in your later letters, is more to me than the success of Solferino. Your freedom comes nearer home to me than the freedom of Italy, much as I desire the latter," are his words. * * * * * The knowledge which he imparted so earnestly, eloquently and unremittingly, from his pen and voice, and from the purchase and distribution, in uncounted numbers, of any books which might further his purpose, he gained at a great cost, and by the exercise of powers of a high philosophic order. * * * * * Whatever might be the theme of his conversation, or the character of the labor he was devising or executing, I felt that I was in the presence of one in whom, although "subject to like passions as we," the desire to be "at one with God," not only regulated powers of vast compass, and sensibilities charged with vitality, but organized and gave unity to a nature of immense volume, so that it was compelled to be constantly useful, on a scale commensurate with its capacity, and yet, so constrained by its own ideals to depreciate itself, that it did the grand work it was called to with seldom an apprehension that it was doing anything. Hence, I have felt that, if he does most for his race who reveals to his fellow-mortals most of the true God, and in such a way that they shall receive and rejoice in the knowledge conferred, Mr. James must ever stand high among the benefactors of his generation. * * * * * His pulpit labors alone were enough to consume the vigor and time of most men. When without a regular ministerial charge, as during the later years of his life, he never hesitated to preach for weeks and weeks, for churches or ministerial brethren whose burdens were heavy. And how did he preach? With the truth so deeply planted, not only in his intellect, but in his sensibilities, it was to be expected that Mr. James would be an impressive preacher. But when it is remembered that his voice was like an organ for depth and compass, and also resonant with feeling; and his mode of composition such that each separate sentence was full of meaning, and closely related to that which went before and followed it—it is not surprising that he reminded many of Robert Hall, in his purity of diction, and in the emphasis of his utterance. He was accustomed to read and meditate much before he wrote, so that his manuscripts contained the invincible judgments of his soul; and his style of speech manifested this. In his conversation, it was often rapid and enthusiastic; from the pulpit, it was more measured. There he spake "as one having authority." No one could hear his discussion of such themes as he presented in his sermons in his exhaustive manner, and not feel that the fire of intense convictions, relating to the life or death of the soul, burned in the breast of him who was giving his thoughts to his hearers.

Remarkable, however, as were his sermons, they were excelled by his devotional exercises. They moved the heart to tears; they rekindled its hope. The mind that in preaching, and in conversation, and in meditation, opened so readily to the being and perfections of God, seemed in prayer to be lifted into His actual presence. Absolved from the ordinary conditions of thought, yet never violating them, Mr. James appeared to absorb the affection of the Creator, and to gain a vision of the ineffable glory as he approached the throne of the heavenly grace. Yet, in that august pavilion, his tones were not those of a stranger, but rather those of one to whom the Lord had been and would be a dwelling-place in all generations. What tenderness, what faith, what adoration were there! What a hiding under the shadow of the Almighty, what communion of the finite with the Infinite, what earnestness of intercession, what a venturing upon the promises! Then it was that he "endured as seeing One who is invisible, and talked with God as a man talketh with his friend."

* * * * * It was a splendid sight to see him from 1852 to 1856, as I did, every summer in Lenox, with his vigorous intellect, his wealth of feeling, his firmly knit frame, his eye that kindled and expanded so immediately as ideal themes were introduced; but it was sublime to know him from 1862 to 1868, after his theology was adjusted, after doubts had ceased to make their appearance, after nature had yielded to the spirit, when every material symbol and every human relationship constantly reminded him of his counterpart in spiritual bonds or Christian joys; when he began to view the things of time from very much the same stand-point that it is supposed redeemed men look at them after they have left the body; when his union with or absorption in God seemed to gain

rapid increase from month to month; and when, without losing a particle of his manly charity and prodigal generosity, and intellectual intrepidity, he seemed ready at any moment (save for that never-satisfied and aching thirst for greater conformity to the Divine mind) to enter upon the employments and enjoyments of immortality.

* * * * * And what shall we say of his friendships? They were formed, in later years especially, somewhat with reference to capacity or need, as he thought, in the subject of them, for spiritual relief and advancement. Was it a soul dark for the want of an apprehension of the mercy of God in Christ, he could not withdraw his affection from it, or his labors.

We need not say that his more intimate friendships were permanent. They could not change nor abate. The fiber of them was eternal; the place for their exercise chiefly beyond the grave. In not a few the memory of him is like the refrain of some great anthem, which increases as it comes back in echoes from the scenes amidst which its notes were struck, and often after the hand which gave them is taken away.

On Saturday night, the 15th of February, 1868, he entered into his rest. Though his sickness had been long, and his sufferings severe, his joy was deep and full. "It is all joy, joy, joy!" were among his last conscious words. Three days before he departed, he said, "My faith is perfect. As I have not produced it I may speak of it thus: It is like the sun, or rather," he continued, "it is like the natural sense we have of the sunlight—quite adequate to reveal the things it is designed to reveal." At another time, when his departure seemed full in view, he said, "The other side is sunny. I call it sunny, because I see only God in the unclouded heavens." * * * "I expect neither surprise nor disappointment in the future. Whatever may be in it, I know that the same God is there whom I have known here, and I trust Him." * * * "My mind is all ready for a shout at the vision of the exceeding glory." * * * "Nothing is so precious to me as that Christ died for us. I hear a voice, saying, 'These are they which have washed their robes and made them white in the blood of the Lamb.'" With such words as these, spontaneously uttered, he was frequently refreshing those who were permitted to watch the shadows departing, while his soul entered more clearly into the dawning and into the day.

Thus he, that in his early days, and in his mature manhood, "thirsted" for holiness, came to the fountain of the River of Life, and to the Paradise of God, where they thirst no more.

"O si sit anima mea cum te."

www.ingramcontent.com/pod-product-compliance
Lightning Source LLC
LaVergne TN
LVHW010207110826
845151LV00002B/624

* 9 7 8 1 4 2 5 5 3 5 4 0 7 *